prison *a symposium*

contributors

EUGENE HEIMLER

PAUL IGNOTUS

RUSSELL BRADDON

ARTHUR KOESTLER

KRISHNA NEHRU HUTHEESING

WALTER MUSGRAVE

COLIN FRANKLIN

JEREMY BRYAN

prison

a symposium
edited by GEORGE MIKES

HORIZON PRESS · NEW YORK

First American edition 1964
Published by Horizon Press, New York
© *Routledge & Kegan Paul* 1963
Library of Congress Catalog Card No. 64-15188

Printed in Great Britain

contents

INTRODUCTION

THIS may be a unique generation, which has so widely felt the full range of suffering. It is common in London or New York to spend evenings in the company of people who were prisoners of the Japanese, of Hitler, of the Hungarian Communists—or of their own stress and breakdown. Prison, in some form, is the symbol of it. This book is an attempt to discover what has been learnt, by those who have known it, of this whole range of prison experience—taking prison to be any form of enforced separation from the world of normal life. Thus there are chapters on mental asylum and hospital, as well as political prison and concentration camp. And the emphasis is on the return rather than the experience. What is the lesson of that time of separation? Having travelled to the end of fear, was it the death of fear—or its exposure? That is the question each author was invited to answer.

Arthur Koestler was sentenced to death by the Nationalists during the Spanish Civil War; Eugene Heimler was sent to the Auschwitz extermination camp by the Nazis; Paul Ignotus was a political prisoner of the Communists in Hungary; Krishna Hutheesing—the only female contributor to this book—was a political prisoner of the British in India; Walter Musgrave spent ten months in a civil prison in England; Russell Braddon was a prisoner of war in a Japanese camp; Colin Franklin spent a year in hospital; Jeremy Bryan was an inmate in a psychiatric ward.

Why do people lock one another up? How does it feel to be caged? How real may such an unreal situation become in time and how unreal does normal, but remote, every-day life seem from behind bars? To what extent does one's past submerge in the humdrum and artificial realities of prison life? What are one's relations with the outside world, with one's jailers and with one-self? Does one feel guilty—even if not of the crime one is alleged to have committed—and can one adjust oneself to one's situation? What scars does such an experience leave? What is it like to come out—does one indeed ever 'come out'? Are we not all prisoners and is not the prisoner inside, with his lack of responsibilities, freer, at least in some respects, than the prisoner outside?

These problems are interesting enough in themselves, but they have a special significance for our age. This era has been called the Age of Anxiety, the Age of Longing and even the Age of the Common Man but it deserves few names better than the Age of Prison. Never in the past have so many people been in prison—most of them innocent people in political captivity; never before has a prison record conferred such distinction as it now does in so many countries; and never before have people exchanged their prison experience so freely, almost boastfully, over black coffee and brandy, in the free lands they have subsequently reached. There is hardly anyone in Central and Eastern Europe who did not lose a relation or a close friend in the Nazi concentration camps; the Communist prisons were full of innocent people during the fifties and they are certainly not empty in the sixties; think of Franco's prisons in Spain, Salazar's in Portugal, Verwoerd's in South Africa, Nkhruma's in Ghana, Mao's in China and all the prisons in the Arab and Caribbean dictatorships. Even this list is far from complete. And to the numbers of those who actually are or were in prison add those who escaped by a hair's breadth—the refugees. Perhaps in no other age were so many languages spoken so badly; perhaps the London of no other age will have such an intimate acquaintance with the broken Central European accent which by now almost ranks as a new dialect of English.

It was not primarily on account of the kind of imprisonment they had suffered that the contributors to this book were chosen.

The first basic problem is, I think, man's relationship with himself; in order to survive one had to save one's self-respect. In itself this was not enough, but without it one perished.

Arthur Koestler made up his mind as soon as his cell-door was locked: he would do exercises every morning, he would learn foreign languages and, most important of all, he would not allow his spirit to be broken. Eugene Heimler survived by visualizing himself as a reporter in Auschwitz: he persuaded himself that he was not just a prisoner but also a chronicler of his time, a Witness. Paul Ignotus preserved his detachment and intellect in the Communist prison, managing to see his guards as miserable, degraded products of the same system that had imprisoned him. Guards, prisoners and the Communist pocket dictators outside were all servants and victims of the same madness. Some suffered physically more than others, but he felt that the A.V.O.—the political police—and their bosses, humiliated themselves more abjectly than they humiliated their prisoners. Russell Braddon saved his self-respect by his sense of humour. He felt it was essential to cheat his guards and prove his own superiority, and perhaps that of all his fellow prisoners, by his minor but important victories. Walter Musgrave also regarded his imprisonment in England as a contest: he arranged an endless series of minor skirmishes for himself and managed to score a sufficient number of victories over the 'screws'—as he always called them even to himself—and the Governor whom he refused to call 'Sir'—the most glorious victory of all. Mrs. Hutheesing needed no ruses or tricks; she went to prison for clear-cut principles. Far from being a victim, she sought incarceration. Being in prison was for her a fulfilment, not a punishment: here we may discern a parallel with the political prisoners of present-day England, the nuclear disarmers. They claim that they are fighting for their principles, in the defence of which they are prepared to suffer imprisonment. That is probably true for many of them. But how many others suffer the principles in order to bask in the glory of imprisonment?

Colin Franklin and Jeremy Bryan were in hospital—
Franklin in a medical, Bryan in a mental institution. Hospitals
are not prisons but their inmates are nevertheless prisoners and
that is why I thought fit to include their experiences in this
volume. You do not have to be guilty to get into hospital but—
as the overwhelming majority of the cases in this book prove—
you do not have to be guilty to get into prison either.

A man in a mental hospital is generally recognized to be a
man deprived of his free will. So he is not 'responsible', in contrast to his fellow-men who are. This line in reasoning, like most
others, leads us back to the problem of free will. We all know
that our will is not free. We can, perhaps, act as we *will* in any
given situation, but we surely cannot *will* differently from the
way we actually do. But to see Man as an automaton, a slave of
circumstance, a creature whose fate is determined by his glands
from the moment of his birth, is an insupportable notion. So we
—whether we are theologians, philosophers or just ordinary
people in instinctive revolt against this intolerable notion—invent
the idea of free will and with it the idea of responsibility. This is
the point where Humanity's self-respect comes in. It is this self-
respect—as artificial or as real as that of any of the prisoners
in this book—which makes it possible for humanity to survive in
its larger prison, called Earth.

The second basic problem is one's attitude to one's own guilt
or innocence. And the first conclusion to which these essays seem
to point is this : the completely innocent person is able to regard
his misfortune as an act of fate. His tragedy is not tragedy in the
classic, Greek sense of the word : it is simply a disaster, neutral
and impersonal, like flood or famine; or like breaking a bone
or catching the plague. It is only his body that is involved : it
was, no doubt, bad luck that it was he who caught the bug or
was thrown into captivity, but no more than bad luck. If he is
guilty, or partially guilty, he is much more personally involved. Through his guilt he becomes his own jailer : he has
locked his own cell-door and does not possess the key to unlock

it. That is unbearable. Jail is a place for the innocent only. Only one among my eight contributors may be regarded as guilty according to the accepted notion of civilized countries; but there are two who *feel* guilty. The two who feel guilty do not include the one who is.

Arthur Koestler does not ever refer to the problem of guilt or innocence—because he assumes he is guilty. He does not question the fact that, in the midst of the Spanish Civil War, he gave ample cause for being sentenced to death. First, he was a 'Red criminal', which meant that he supported the Republican side (his connections with the Communist Party were unknown at the time); he was also a 'traitor' because during a previous visit to Franco's headquarters, he had had plenty of opportunity to observe how much German and Italian military support there was for the insurgents. He did not spy; he took no photographs; he made no sketches. Indeed, he saw no more than what was freely and proudly displayed to Nazi, Fascist and other right-wing journalists. His worst crime, however, was his interview with General Queipo de Llano, as the general, by granting the interview, made a fool of himself. To die for such crimes seems preposterous in the comparative sobriety of the Cold War and at a distance of a quarter of a century; it seemed only too well merited, almost just, in the middle thirties.

Koestler was not trapped by the nationalists or by ill luck. As readers of his *Spanish Testament*[1] and his autobiography[2] know : he sat down and waited for them. He courted disaster, fully aware that Franco's political police were searching for him with furious zest. He wanted to die, although he never quite admits it. Whether he was just tired of the futile struggle inside and outside Spain, or whether his overwhelming and everlasting feeling of guilt compelled him to accept punishment for the

[1] *Spanish Testament* (Victor Gollancz, 1937), reissued, in abbreviated form, under the title of *Dialogue with Death*, Collins and Hamish Hamilton, 1954 and Grey Arrow Books, 1961, from which the essay published here has been condensed.
[2] *The Invisible Writing* (Collins and Hamish Hamilton, 1954).

guilt of his Party, for the Left, and for the folly of humanity, I
cannot tell. He certainly did not feel guilty 'in the sense of the
indictment'—particularly as there was no indictment.

He *feared* death, too. Death, as he remarks, is a very personal
matter; it is also forbiddingly final. Hatred of life is not in-
compatible with fear of death : they go arm in arm. An abstract
death-wish—an emotional urge to end it all—is one thing; to be
dragged out of a cell and driven away on a lorry at dawn to
face a very concrete firing squad is quite another.

This frightful experience, he says elsewhere, made a life-long
impression on him. But one has the feeling that the experience
created nothing new : it was created, in fact, by Koestler's own
desperate and admirable desire to participate; to see hell as others
see it and suffer for his own cause when others suffer—and also
by the tragic, disillusioned, yet passionately idealistic view of
life. The experience only underlined certain feelings.

No inmate of any prison can be more innocent than a prisoner
of war, yet Russell Braddon is the only other contributor to this
volume who is tormented by a feeling of guilt. He tells us in
his remarkable and otherwise almost light-hearted essay that he
suffered the 'abject humiliation' of surrender, in asking for
mercy from an enemy, whom an instant earlier, he would have
slaughtered without compunction. The alternative, however,
would have been to continue a hopeless struggle and sacrifice his
life for no purpose. Braddon's feelings are the noble emotions of
a sensitive soul; but they reflect the spirit of Japanese *bushido*
rather than the less heroic and more commonsense morality of
today's Christian Europe. His concern in a small, innocent and
creditable way reflects one of the gravest dangers of
imprisonment : the prisoner may come to resemble his jailers.
We become similar to *them*.

The only contributor who may justly be regarded as guilty is
Walter Musgrave (a pseudonym). He was sent to prison for ob-
taining credit while bankrupt. At the time of his trial he was in
a desperate, almost suicidal, mood, for reasons which had only

little to do with the proceedings. Today he is convinced that he was ill-advised to plead guilty and to consent to be tried by magistrates, instead of a judge and jury. He thinks he would have escaped much more lightly and he is probably right. However, he did, in fact, plead guilty and is the only one of the contributors who is burning with resentment and feels more sinned against than sinner.

The reason for this is not difficult to discern. Firstly resentment is a human feeling. You do not feel resentment against flood, fire or a gale, nor against a snake that bites you, but only against fellow-humans, with whom you have a great deal in common. If you have caught an illness—you fight it; you do your best to overcome it and prove stronger than the disease but you do not feel any personal hatred of the bacilli. The S.S. or the A.V.O. put themselves beyond the pale of humanity : they were the bacilli of a mad, sick age. A.V.O. men recognized during the Hungarian Revolution of 1956 were strung up on the first tree or lamp-post without the slightest compunction. But this was a political act : it was the A.V.O. as an institution that was hanged—repeatedly : individual A.V.O. agents were, as a rule, unknown to the avengers. Inmates of the Nazi concentration camps or Communist prisons may have burned with Gargantuan hatred, with Biblical loathing, may have been consumed by a fire, acerbity and abhorrence worthy of King Lear—but they could not have been tormented by the petty, human, almost cosy feeling of resentment.

Secondly, resentment results from a sense of injustice. This problem does not even arise for the victims of Nazi camps and Communist prisons—in the cases of Heimler and Ignotus. It was sheer, sadistic madness to lock up Heimler and Ignotus; it was an unpleasant but undisputed necessity to keep Russell Braddon in a P.O.W. camp; it was Krishna Hutheesing herself who courted imprisonment as a follower of Gandhi; but Musgrave was supposed to pay a debt he owed to society. And he has a strong feeling that he overpaid his debt—even if his sentence was just and no more than he deserved. Having paid his debt fully, having suffered the punishment meted out to him, he left prison (with £2 in his pocket), a ruined, broken man. His reputation was gone, his past wiped out and his future bleak. Most of his family had turned against him and with no money to feed himself properly he actually often went hungry, in spite of some help from the National Assistance Board. His old friends and acquaintances now seemed remote, mythical figures belonging to another world. Received everywhere with suspicion, sneaking contempt and whispers—or at least sensing these things even when they were non-existent—he justly feels that his punishment did not end but, indeed only began when the prison gates were opened to let him out. In this sense, *every* prison sentence is unjust. To incarcerate a violent and dangerous criminal for the protection of society is clearly unavoidable; but to imprison mild, weak, erratic and fallen men for a few months and *for punishment* is surely wrong as long as *being in prison* is much less of a punishment than *having been in prison*.

Not that being in prison is sheer joy. It is not meant to be but it is not meant to be torture and humiliation either. A person is not sent to prison to be punished there; he is sent to prison *as* punishment. The confinement is the punishment.

Inmates of a civil prison are not outcasts and pariahs like inmates of a Nazi concentration camp or a Communist prison : they are members of the society which condemns them. And that is exactly what makes their punishment effective; that is exactly why their position is so hard to bear. It is not a feared and hated enemy of their race, religion, nation or political creed who treads them down but their own fellows. But for the grace of God, they feel, they might be guarding their warders. They accept the verdict of society—after all, it is in a sense their own verdict—but resent what they feel to be the petty tyranny of small officials. For the inmates of a concentration camp the immediate menace was the S.S. thug in charge but they were,

in fact, hired murderers only; the real enemy was the powers
behind and far above the S.S. men—powers and forces of insanity and wickedness with whom the prisoner had nothing in
common. The political prisoners' bitterness remains an ideo-
logical bitterness, and he has some moral capital to fall back
upon; the short-term civil prisoner's bitterness (long-term
prisoners are a different problem altogether, representing an
entirely different attitude to prison and prison-officials) is necessarily reduced to a trivial, perhaps warm and personal level. He
has passed sentence on himself : every citizen is a member of
every jury in the land. But as this contention—the contention of
his own responsibility—is unacceptable to him, the prison
warders and the governor become symbols of his own guilt and
failure, they become villains and the fight is on.

Walter Musgrave is a cultured, highly intelligent and pleasant,
if somewhat pugnacious man. When I asked—referring to a
story he had just told me—why some people, nearing release,
still escape, although it is clear that when recaptured—as recaptured they nearly alway are—they lose more time in can-
celled remission than they would gain with escape, he looked at
me in complete stupefaction : 'But don't you understand? One
doesn't escape to gain freedom. One escapes to beat *them*. You
must beat them.' Yes, it is *we* and *they*. We, the prisoners are
always right and on the side of the angels; they, the prison
official are always wrong and all villains.

Prisons are as old as humanity. Ever since Cain and Abel one
man has always tried to enslave another and exert power over
him. No one is more fully in your power than your prisoner.

Some people become warders—or prison officers as they are
now termed—from noble and altruistic motives; for others it is
simply a job—they might equally well have become park attend-
ants, factory foremen or greengrocers. But there can be no
doubt that a considerable percentage choose this calling simply
because they enjoy having power over their fellow-men. This
caesaromania develops after a time—in more or less degree—in

most prison warders, whatever their original motive for joining the service may have been. It is a professional deformity : all professions and jobs—shop-steward or teacher, nurse or sergeant major—carry the built-in risks of their own special type of deformity.

Being a prison warder is, of course, an extremely difficult job, needing an exceptional amount of wisdom and good temper, a sense of humour or at least sense of proportion, and a good understanding of human nature. The warder is bound to come across many insecure, perturbed, frightened and mentally unbalanced people whose troubles bubble to the surface in the form of aggressiveness or violence. He also meets with a great deal of genuine nastiness, vindictiveness and bloody-mindedness—not all criminals are, after all, pure angels, contrary to a modern belief which is gaining more and more ground. Even the most patient and idealistically minded prison officer will meet so many rebuffs, disappointments and cases of misplaced trust, that he will gradually be driven to the conclusion that toughness is the only sensible policy. The former idealists will be pushed nearer and nearer to the little Caesars, pocket Hitlers and turnkey-tyrants. This is—as Spencer called it—the 'constitution of things'—and it cannot be helped as long as society imprisons people for punishment, as long as prison officers remain human, and as long as many prisoners remain subnormal—in need of medical care rather than judicial retribution.

If there is a fear of death in us, there is also a death-wish. If we find sadists in our midst, we also find masochists. If we find people who desire to rule over others and make their fellows slaves, we find many who insist on being knocked around and being slaves. If there exists a desire to imprison others, there also exists a desire to be imprisoned by others—the prison-wish.

Freud quarrelled with one of his early disciples, Otto Rank, because of Rank's theory of the birth trauma. This idea was first developed in Rank's book, *The Trauma of Birth,* published in 1923. Rank wanted to out-Freud Freud and maintained that the decisive influences in a man's life were not those of early childhood but those of birth. The trauma of birth—the release from the safety of the mother's womb he held to be the cause of all the neuroses of later life; the cure would be to produce a transference situation, resulting in rebirth. Rank's theory was no serious discovery; it never had any significant following and it died an early death. Ernest Jones remarked : 'It accorded with the hypomanic phase through which Rank was then passing. No data were given which could be tested, and most of the book consisted of extravagant speculations in the field of art, philosophy and religion.'[1]

I am not trying to revive Rank's long-dead theory, nor am I trying to base any further theories on it—I am not qualified to invent any theories. But using Rank's idea simply as a basis for a simile : is there not a strong parallel between the birth-trauma and the release-from-prison trauma? Is one not protected and looked after in prison, relieved of all responsibility—in fact, spoilt in a perverse and crude fashion—and shielded from a hostile, outside world? Is it not possible that some people identify prison with the mother's womb—a dark, lonely and cheerless, yet secure and quiet place? Could this identification be one of the sources of the prison-wish?

The other source—and this theory is much more widely accepted—is that of guilt. People desire to go to prison because they feel guilty (although never, or hardly ever, for the crime they are charged with) and wish to punish themselves. The two theories are not mutually exclusive. Both desires have the same, ultimate aim—to be imprisoned; they are, however, different in origin and character.

Whatever the reason, the prison-wish does exist and three of our contributors could easily have escaped prison, had they chosen to do so. Mrs. Krishna Hutheesing was a follower of Mahatma Gandhi's civil disobedience campaign and went to

[1] Ernest Jones: *Sigmund Freud, Life and Work*, Vol. III, The Hogarth Press, 1957.

2

prison because Gandhi had ordered his followers to get themselves arrested. In the nationalistic upsurge of the time, her actions and motives can be easily understood. But the cases of Arthur Koestler and Paul Ignotus are more complex. Koestler allowed himself to be arrested in Malaga when he had ample opportunity to get away and in spite of the fact that he knew he was a wanted man. Paul Ignotus, having spent the war years in the employment of the B.B.C., was the press-attaché of the Hungarian Legation in London when, in the perilous and mad times following Rajk's arrest, in the late forties, he returned to Budapest of his own free will. It is not that he was recalled and obeyed orders; *he insisted on being re-called*. His friends—myself among them—pointed out the dangers of which, of course, he himself was fully aware. Yet he went—and subsequently spent nearly seven years in prison. Why?

He tried to convince us and himself that he wanted to see his father, who was fatally ill, once more. Perhaps theories about prison-wish à la Rank's birth-trauma are as far-fetched as are such simple rationalizations and, possibly, the old, trite, yet often proved theory of guilt-feeling and self-punishment are nearer to the truth. But why—for what imaginary crimes—did he want to punish himself—and punish himself so severely, we shall probably never know. Nor will he.

Once having been in prison, can anyone ever come out or does one carry one's own prison cell around forever? I do not speak, of course, of habitual criminals, for whom prison is as normal a professional risk as loss on the stock-exchange is for a speculator or the risk of infection for a general practitioner. I am speaking of people, like the contributors to this book, for whom prison—until they found themselves inside—existed only on a different, remote plane and for whom being in prison meant, or seemed to mean, a complete collapse of their lives. Walter Musgrave was, in one respect, in the easiest position of them all : he knew all the time exactly when he would be allowed to leave. Mrs. Hutheesing's position was worse but she was surely convinced that her imprisonment, harsh though it was, would not last indefinitely. But Russell Braddon in his Japanese P.O.W. camp and even more, Paul Ignotus, in a Hungarian, Communist prison must have wondered if they would ever know freedom and life again. The odds, for these two, were perhaps about evenly balanced, and they must have been torn between hope and despair, depending partly on their own emotional ups and downs and on such scanty news as reached them from the outside world. Eugene Heimler in spite of his brave optimism, must often have felt that the odds were heavily against him and that his chances of survival were infinitesimal—as indeed they were. Arthur Koestler probably *knew* that he had reached journey's end. Such experiences, of course, cannot disappear from a man's life as a small cloud disappears. They cause shocks that most of us, more fortunate, never experience and are unable to comprehend. They leave deep wounds which appear to heal slowly with time, but remain permanent—though invisible. I am reminded of professional boxers who suffer innumerable but (in their lifetime) undetectable minor haemorrhages: no one quite knows what damage these haemorrhages do to the brain but it cannot be slight.

I knew an ex-inmate of a Nazi concentration camp who, formerly a tall and well developed if rather thin, sporting type of a man, weighed 5 stones 11 pounds on his release. When he came to London he could not stop eating: by the time he left for New York—about eight months after his arrival here—he had regained his normal weight. I saw him four years later again in America, when he weighed just under 17 stones—and he still could not stop eating. 'I'll eat myself to death,' he told me repeatedly and he did. In the mid-fifties he died of heart trouble, due to over-eating. Such clear-cut, almost indecently plain and over-emphatic case-book histories are rare. To many people it seemed that this man had survived the harshness of the concentration camp but succumbed to the lush temptations of a free and prosperous world. This is, of course, nonsense. My poor friend was a direct victim of the cruelty and privations of camp-life.

Yet, in spite of the visible chips on the shoulder and the invisble scars at the bottom of one's soul, imprisonment does not seem to change a man's basic character. Early 1947 another survivor of Belsen came to see me in London and we had a long talk about life and death. He told me that he regarded his survival as not only a miracle but as a sheer gift from God : he ought to have died a thousand times, he explained, and his remaining alive was a generous present of Fate. This feeling, he went on, had taught him humility; he was satisfied with his lot and would remain content whatever was in store for him : everything was better than Belsen. I tried to talk him out of this abject and humble attitude but was completely unsuccessful. The next time I met him was in a Hungarian restaurant in Soho. We were not supposed to be lunching together but by chance we both arrived very early and I heard him quarrelling bitterly with the head-waiter because he had not been given a corner-table. How could anyone expect him to lunch at that miserable, uncomfortable little table in the middle of the room?

I thought of this very often—perhaps more often than the significance of this little story warrants. Does this mean that some people, whatever happens to them and whatever pious resolutions they make, are unable to learn even from the most shattering, murderous experiences? Or am I wrong again and was I, once again, catching a glimpse of one of those hidden scars? Perhaps if he had never been in Belsen, he would have accepted without a murmur that uncomfortable little table in the middle of the room.

I very much hope that the reader, having finished this volume, will know a great deal more about prison experience, its significance and its effects than he knew before starting it. I am convinced that this book—unsystematic as it has deliberately been left—adds up to an often overwhelming, often puzzling picture. In my view much of it is excellent writing and it can stand on its own feet as prison literature. If the book poses almost as many questions as it solves—or if different contributors answer the same question in their own, different ways—I believe this is not a fault of this book. It simply reminds us that some questions have many answers; some have none. And that often we are simply groping.

I have to add that I myself have never been in prison. I was chosen to edit this volume, as the publisher has kindly put it, because he thought I knew how to edit a book. This was a simple, if courteous reference to the fact that I am a first-class bureaucrat, who conscientiously answers letters, searches out the right people as contributors and then prods them with gentle persistence to keep to deadlines—more or less. My present preface is intended to describe only the book's aims and is based, mostly on points arising from the manuscripts.

Some of my friends urged me to go and see a prison at least as a visitor, before writing this preface. This advice seemed sensible and well-meant; nevertheless, I was unable to follow it.

Prison visitors are admirable people and even if their number includes a small percentage of curious fools and determined do-gooders, they are on the whole doing a worthwhile and sisyphean job well. They have my admiration; but I could not persuade myself to visit a prison. I should feel like a visitor in a human zoo; curiosity—just to see what it is like—is not sufficient justification. There is even—I felt—an element of gloating in it : who could, after all, fail to say to himself at the sight of all those wretched prisoners : 'I'll walk out in an hour's time and you'll stay here.' And who could fail to read the same thoughts in their eyes.

No. If I go to prison, I shall have to go as a prisoner, not a visitor.

GEORGE MIKES

CHILDREN OF AUSCHWITZ

By Eugene Heimler

WHEN on the 4th April, 1944 I appeared on the streets
of my home town, Szombathely (Western Hungary), wearing
the Star of David on my jacket for the first time, I knew that
in more than one sense I had stepped back into the Middle
Ages. That morning's issue of the local newspaper advised its
Gentile readers, when they saw the Yellow Star, to ignore its
wearers as though they did not exist; and the Editor in his
leader quoted the past with reference to historical justice, saying
that the yellow badge was almost as old as Christianity itself.

He was right, of course. In 1215 Pope Innocent III convened
the Fourth Lateran Council in Rome, at which it was unani-
mously agreed that henceforth Jews must wear a badge on their
clothing like lepers and prostitutes.

'The Fourth Lateran Council settled the destiny of the Jewish
people for many centuries. They continued to wander over the
face of the earth, without rights, except by gracious concession,
without a home, and without security; treated at all times in
years of peace and in years of persecution as if they were beings
of an inferior species.'[1]

On that April day, American bombers were flying across the
distant northern sky, and as I watched the white trails they left
behind them, they were the only visible reminder to me, a Jew,

---

[1] Malcolm Hay; *Europe and the Jews*, Beacon Press, Boston, U.S.A.

that this was indeed the Twentieth Century. That morning, as
if drawn by an invisible magnet, many of us gathered together
in the old synagogue. The discussion was concerned, strangely
enough, not with the future, or with the present, but mainly with
the past. Our chief concern, it seemed, was to establish a prece-
dent, as we surrounded the bearded Jews who stood in their
picturesque traditional clothing, the eternal talmudists of all time.

'We shall survive,' they said, 'because none of this is new.'

'You remember,' one old man asked, 'when we were exiled to
Babylon?'

'Of course we remember.'

'Well, did we not succeed in the end, not only in remaining
alive but also in spreading His words to the pagans?'

Looking back, that conversation now seems ridiculous. We
talked as if the past were present and the present in the past. Why
did we tolerate this degradation and all that followed subsequently? The answer may be found in the conditioning of our
minds. We argued that, if we had survived Babylon and Assyria,
Rome and Spain, we should certainly survive Hitler. We took into
consideration the spasmodic pogroms of the past, of course, but
history had never taught us the possibility of total annihilation :
we had never experienced an Auschwitz, or the gas chambers.

Despite this, some of us young men and women were in a
dangerous mood then. We knew that within a month we should
have to enter the town ghetto, and some of us seriously considered burning it down before that time. We thought that if we
started a fire of defiance in our home town it might spread to
other towns and would call the attention of the world to our
plight. But our elders disapproved, saying that these dangerous
times called for level heads, that our chief weapon did not consist of violence. They even went so far as to say that it would be
unjewish to risk the lives of any Gentiles who might disapprove
of national socialism.

In those days family ties still bore the mark of the Nineteenth
Century; and being in a feudal land, we felt little of the impact

of the great industrial age on our personal lives. Father was still a patriarch, and the 'old wise men' were still clothed in the magic that was their heritage of bygone centuries. So the rebellion in our minds remained a secret one.

The Yellow Star in 1944 was intended to degrade us, just as it had been meant to degrade us in 1215. 'It is evident that the wearing of this badge was not intended to encourage Catholics to seek their company.'[1] The words referring to those early days still held true. In fact, the Yellow Star was the first phase in the process of extermination. It divided the world into two halves, theirs and ours. And between the two was an evergrowing empty space. Personal contacts were severed; it was now dangerous for a Gentile to walk down the street with a Jew. Our pride hurt, we could be nothing but proud, sometimes with reason, and sometimes without.

By the end of April I became aware of an uncanny feeling of being closed in, not by bars or guards, but by those who lived in that other half of the world. I felt as if I were in a cage, and night after night I dreamed of breaking out.

When I approached the Bishop of our town to help some of us young people by allowing us to work on his estate at a time when we were not allowed by law to do any work, he looked at us blankly. His eyes were dead, but his words conveyed a different message:

'The Church cannot help you . . . none of you . . . unless you become one of us . . . But I shall pray for you, my children. . . .'

The loneliness of those days was intolerable. It was early spring, and I remember how I watched the wind gathering into a heap the fragments of dust from the pavement and then with a sudden cold gust, whirling them away. This image, as if it had been a projection of our fate, has remained with me ever since.

*   *   *

[1] Joseph Bonsirven, *Juifs et Chretiens*, p. 47.

The fear of reality can never be as frightening as the fear of the unknown. Within the walls of the ghetto, the oldest and most neglected part of our town, four thousand human beings lived under conditions that are impossible to describe; while in the offices of the Jewish Council counter-espionage agents were torturing people to disclose where they had hidden their money and valuables. To accept all this passively was frightening enough, but the real fear came from an unknown source. We knew by now that our days on Hungarian soil were numbered, and some even spoke of imminent death, yet we could not believe it. Deportation and exile were not new in our history, but beneath the surface of rumour we sensed some impending threat that like a tidal wave attacked our consciousness and paralysed us into inactivity.

Men and women reached out towards each other in vain. Love had become a last desperate attempt to find peace, but fear was playing strange tricks with our sexual desires. We craved for unity, yet at the height of the moment the candle flickered out and there was nothing but darkness. At night I used to walk a lot and listen, self-appointed chronicler of those times. There was no privacy, and the ear could catch words never meant for strangers.

As I walked those streets I thought of the many personal tragedies that this new pattern of ghetto life had imposed on all of us. A few miles away, the normal world was moving along its usual course; the established classes were living as before, the church bells rang for litany, and the shops served their customers: business as usual. But in our world things were different. We were all Jews, of course, but what did it mean to be a Jew? Apart from the common tradition that united us, our broken class structure clearly indicated that we no longer belonged to the established order. During these weeks the Jewish lawyer, doctor, architect were thrown together into one home, often into one room, with the Jewish baker, merchant, and traveller in underwear. The clash of habits, values and customs was intensified by this new ghetto existence. It had never occurred to me until then that Jews were not a homogenous group; and in this artificial world it was easy to be hopeless about the future of a Jewish state. Now that we had lost our accustomed civilization, it did not take long to sink into a form of existence where nothing mattered but the survival of the self.

My pride was broken by this discovery. Once one tolerates the Yellow Star, the ghetto, the tortures in the Council offices, one is no longer a man. And when self-respect is lost, then faith is lost, and when faith is lost, man becomes a number without a name.

In the end it was not the Marxists, the Zionists, the learned professionals who kept the torch burning in their shaking hands; it was the Chassidic Jews, and in comparison with these giants one could feel one's true insignificance. It was not we, the writers, the artists, the doctors and the philosophers, who had preserved Jewry throughout the centuries, but these people, unchanged from the beginning of Jewish history, singing the songs of Zion now not by the waters of Babylon but in the ghetto of Szombathely.

The segregation of the criminal for the sake of society is essential. The rights and safety of the citizen must be protected. Segregation however is one thing : punishment is another. Segregation implies a logical necessity, punishment conveys the idea of retribution. Punishment can never be effective in helping the prisoner in his emotional growth. It can have the opposite effect, and it may make him more immature and more hostile than he was at the time of his crime.

Throughout the long journey towards maturity, it is the parent's task to control the child. This task is undertaken, in ordinary conditions, through love, and punishment is an aspect of this love. The child reacts to punishment and mends his ways, not because of the physical or emotional pain, but because he loves his parents. There can be no love between the State and the citizen. The birch and the cane may release our own anger and aggression, it may even control the behaviour of some through fear of repetition, but it can never teach a person humanity.

But what happens if the prisoner has committed no crime; if he finds himself locked up, tortured and beaten, knowing his own innocence? How can he cope with this world? Can he remain sane if he continues to bang his head against the prison walls? Or will he in the end believe that he has committed the crime that he was charged with and what price will he have to pay for this delusion? Will he try to find another reason for being in jail, not the one he was accused of, but one that he may fabricate to endure his life?

The predicament of the Jew in German concentration camps was greater than that of the criminal or political prisoner. Those knew why they had been sent there : they had done something. The Jew had done nothing. Within weeks of our arrival in Auschwitz three groups emerged among these Jewish inmates. The first group complained : 'They have done this to us and we have done nothing to deserve it.' These people, surrounded by the electrified wire, felt bewildered and lost. Very few of them survived. The second group consisted of Jews who found a reason for being there. 'We are here because we are Jews.' To them being a Jew had a special significance. They were usually fanatics and uncompromising followers of their faith, or ardent believers in Zion in the nationalistic sense. Quite a number of these people survived. The third group, to which I belonged, was able to find a personal meaning in living.

I soon discovered that life or death depended not only on chance, but also on whether or not one could find a meaning to one's life. This was of course no safeguard against the gas chambers, or the bullets of the S.S. It only meant that if one was lucky enough to avoid these, one was protected from the many other dangers that threatened one's life, mainly from within. I was twenty-two years old at that time, and I had given little previous thought to the problem of whether or not there was a meaning in life. Most of my fellow prisoners had already found some meaning in their past lives. Many perhaps had never put it into words, yet their past actions clearly indicated a standard of values. Some had found their purpose in family life, some in professional work, some in business, some in distant dreams. But all meaning in the past was now meaningless. I had to find a meaning to my life for the first time—in, of all places, Auschwitz. Unlike those of my fellow Jews who believed in the eternal, invisible, and mighty God of Israel, I was now unable to believe in a God when night after night thousands were burned at the modern stake. The concept of 'God our Father' was consumed in the crematorium along with the flesh of my relatives and friends.

At home I had always dreamed of being a poet; in fact, I had written and published some poems before and during the war. I had dreamed that I should one day be a famous writer. It was in the ghetto, however, that I first appointed myself a chronicler of our times. Now in Auschwitz that temporary appointment was confirmed, and gave a new meaning to my life : to become an eye witness, a writer without pen who registers everything so that one day he can tell the world what he has seen on behalf of the millions who can no longer speak or write. This purpose became a bridge between my past dreams and the future. It was important, because there had to be a future for life to have any meaning.

Dr. Bruno Bettelheim in his brilliant study on concentration camp life says this about the meaning of his life in the concentration camp :

'While swapping tales that evening, it suddenly flashed through my mind that "this is driving me crazy", and I felt that if I were to go on that way, I would in fact end up crazy. That was when I decided that rather than be taken in by such rumours I would try to understand what was psychologically behind them. . . .'

'. . . Thus my interest in trying to understand psychologically is an example of a spontaneous defence against the impact of an extreme situation. It was individually conceived, was neither enforced by the S.S. nor suggested by other prisoners, and was based on my particular background and training. Although at first I was only dimly aware of this, it was meant to protect me from a disintegration of personality I dreaded.'[1]

I cannot say that my newly found meaning remained always in the focus of my consciousness. There were times of pain and horror in which I forgot it completely. Yet it recurred again and again. It was a private victory, too, over the S.S. guards, who never knew that I had them under observation.

The problem of sanity and survival was greatly linked with the question of freedom, or rather the loss of it. That in the concentration camps the area of personal freedom was reduced to a minimum, or even to nothing, is now common knowledge. Imprisonment of any kind means loss of freedom, but it has its degrees. An ordinary prisoner in an ordinary jail still has some limited contact with the world outside; he may write and receive letters, see relatives, read newspapers and books. He is also free to think about his loved ones as he pictures them in familiar surroundings. But in the concentration camp none of these 'Freedoms' were available. Even freedom to think about one's relatives was tinged with such anxiety and fear that the emotional pain over their uncertain fate prohibited memory. In a very real sense, many lived without a past and without a future.

A man who steps out of the dimension of past and future can only live for the present. As he is now conditioned neither by tradition nor ambition, he will become a satellite of the moment and move in a new orbit. He will either die or he will become an instrument in the hand of the S.S., shaped to their image. Now he will kill his comrades without any feeling of guilt, will torture, rape or steal. The gods of the underworld sanction his actions, even approve of them. It is their approval that keeps him going.

In the camp was a doctor of medicine whom I had known in the old days. He had been a most humane man, well liked and

[1] Bruno Bettelheim; *The Informed Heart*, Thames & Hudson, 1961, p. 112.

respected by all. If anyone had told me that one day this man would have a whip in his hand, and would use it against his former friends and patients, I would have thought him mad; and yet in the camp, after only a few weeks, this is what happened when the doctor was put in charge of a barrack. Some psychologists would conclude that Dr. X had had this in him all the time, but that now there was an opportunity to express his sadism. Perhaps we do all have sadistic tendencies, yet not all of us would give free vent to this destructive emotion. It may well be that Dr. X was merely a man whose bridge to his past had been blown up by the S.S., and in order to survive he was forced to live for the present according to the laws of the present. In an emotional vacuum there is no reality except that of the present. The following remarks were made to me by a fellow prisoner in the summer of 1944, in the concentration camp of Troglitz :

'Jancsi, lad, what do you think determines the destiny of a man? What does it depend on, whether one is dragged down by suffering, or raised to a higher level by it? Biochemists attribute it all to hormones, psychologists to early unresolved conflicts, sociologists put everything down to poverty and unsatisfactory working conditions. Have a look round. How many of these people did you know back home? Quite a number. Of the good ones, how many have remained good? And how many of them who used to be bad have become human beings here? The concentration camps have created a civilization within a civilization. And in this new civilization the truths and laws whose validity we believed in for centuries have been turned upside down. You, Jancsi, if you compare these two "civilizations", don't you find yourself compelled to conclude that the people who under these abnormal circumstances manage to prove themselves human are not necessarily those who can do so outside the prison bars? And if you can see an answer to this problem, tell me : on what does it depend whether a man remains a man?'

After eighteen years, I think I can supply the answer to my dead comrade. First, it depends on one's capacity to have faith, to maintain a traditional link with one's past; and secondly on an ability to find a meaning to one's life, which will form a bridge between the past and future.

In Auschwitz I saw no children in the camp, at least no Jewish children. (In the gypsy camp, until their final extermination in July, 1944, children did live with their families.) Any small Jewish child was murdered in the gas-chambers with his mother on arrival. Later, however, during the summer and autumn of 1944, I met a few children in the camp at Buchenwald; and I was in charge of sixteen of them during the winter and early spring in the camp of Berga-Elster, when I headed a group of potato-peelers in the camp kitchen. Although these children were now in their early 'teens, many of them had been deported to various camps many years before. How they had managed to survive, I don't know, but I do know that the political prisoners in Buchenwald looked after them once they were there, and that some even risked their lives for them.

From December until April I spent ten hours every day with them while peeling potatoes. We were warm sitting by the huge pots, and if we felt hungry there was always some boiled potato to be had with a little margarine. The children came originally from many different countries in Europe: Russia, Poland, Germany, Czechoslovakia, Rumania, Hungary, Yugoslavia. By now they all spoke German, the language of the enemy. At first they were suspicious of my motives for being 'nice' to them. The perverse wickedness of the Nazi machinery had managed to paralyse their youthful souls, transforming them into cold little machines who looked for a self-interested motive behind every human act. A person who showed them kindness must therefore be either a homosexual with designs on their bodies or a Nazi spy wanting to use them as informers. The ten-year-olds could still cry, but not those of fourteen, who were impudent, bullying and sometimes dangerous.

Apart from a genuine fondness for these children and a desire to help them, I was also interested in them as a writer. I was motivated by a desire to learn as much about their thoughts and feelings as possible, for I did not know of any other phase of recent history in which small children had been put behind prison bars and completely cut off from the influence of an organized society. More than half of these children had been toddlers when their parents were killed or imprisoned, and they had witnessed horrors of a magnitude that surpasses human imagination.

The children in Berga-Elster soon realized that their protector was neither a homosexual nor a Nazi spy, and the hours we spent together among the ovens drew us all nearer to each other. Their young minds, thirsty for knowledge, looked to me for answers to the many questions which, during the nightmarish course of the past years, they had not even learnt to formulate. We talked about God, about democracy, about the world we hoped for after the war—a world where one would have enough to eat and be able to roam the streets freely, where everybody would be able to think what he liked and say what he thought. In the long nights we spoke at times about the worlds beyond the world, about the stars whose light must travel for millions of years before reaching our earth. We wondered if there was life on the planets that we saw sparkling in the frozen night through the kitchen windows. They continually asked me if there had ever been in the history of mankind a time such as this, whether there had ever lived other Hitlers who had destroyed people in their fiery furnaces. They inquired about the differences between Judaism and Christianity, and whether Jesus was really the Son of God. Their instructors in Buchenwald had not discussed any of these questions with them.

At first they asked the questions, and I, to the best of my ability, tried to supply the answers; but soon I started to ask them questions, and it was then that I learned something about the inner experiences of children in concentration camps.

Unlike the adults, whose memory was badly disturbed during

imprisonment, these children could remember a very great deal, although the memory was sometimes isolated, like a fragment of a broken mirror. One boy of ten talked thus about his father and mother : 'I remember the Man lifting me up, and kissing my face; I remember the Woman watching and saying something to him.' This boy had been deported to Theresienstadt with 'the man and the woman', and for some time he could not say 'father' or 'mother'. 'The Man was beaten there by the S.S., he was kicked to the ground, and he just lay there doing nothing. He didn't hit back. No, the Man didn't hit back. He should have hit back, but he didn't.'

There was something very eery about this kind of recollection, as if the humiliation of the father had to be denied, as if the word 'Man' was easier to endure than to say : 'My father didn't hit back.'

These children did not play the usual childish games of 'Cowboys and Indians'. Some, when I explained what such games were about, said that they were 'silly' or 'disgusting'. They did not play with tin soldiers or their equivalent. Their game was 'to watch'. I asked them what they were watching. At first they were rather reluctant to disclose the information, but eventually it became clear that they 'liked watching the S.S.-man.'

'Watching the S.S., what for ?'

Then it dawned on me that what they liked watching was the cruelty and sadism of the S.S. They watched them beat people, kick people, torture people, kill people. Indeed, they needed no aggressive play. Reality mirrored their phantasy life. What other children in normal society act out through play, these children *witnessed in reality*. And if play was absent, guilt over aggression seemed also absent. If another child annoyed them, they would attack viciously, not restraining themselves in any way, kicking any part of the body without consideration for the damage caused. It soon became clear to me that they were modelling themselves on the S.S.; that, whether secret or proclaimed, the ambition of their lives was to become like the S.S.

Most of these children never formed an enduring relationship with an adult, or became particularly fond of anyone. But I remember two episodes that I considered at the time significant. One day while working in the kitchen I had a slight fainting attack, and was sick. This was soon after we had started working together. Although I could hardly walk to the door, not one of them offered any help; they just sat there peeling potatoes, as if I was no concern of theirs. Had I died then, they would have carried on as usual. Months later, I cut my thumb while peeling potatoes, and at once a number of them came forward to assist me. When this particular period was reached, a number of these children seemed much more depressed about what the S.S. did 'out there' than ever before. Some also complained of having nightmares, something that had seldom happened to them before. It seems as though their feeling of guilt increased as they began to form relationships. When the camp was finally evacuated, and we started on a long march back, these children stuck to me as if I were their father or brother, and they were not only helpful to me, but to some extent to each other too.

It has been asked why prisoners did not rebel against the S.S., why they endured tortures without protest. There were, in fact, spasmodic acts of resistance, like the famous revolt of the Sonderkommando of the Crematorium in Auschwitz, when a number of S.S. men were killed, but on the whole such opposition was very rare. The reasons for this are manifold, but the main one was the emotional state of the prisoners, a condition difficult to understand by people who have never been in concentration camps.

The brutality of the S.S., separation from loved ones, lack of food and sleep, exhaustion, the constant threat to life, the loss of familiar patterns of the past and uncertainty about the future created an emotional state very similar to that of the human infant, who, entering a strange new world, reacts instinctively to the many dangers that threaten from within and without. It is through the infant's relationship to his mother that he learns to love, to acquire a sense of security and in time a sense of reality.

It is through this relationship that our inner and outer worlds achieve separation, and we emerge from the process as individuals.

In the camps a carefully planned policy which aimed at de-individualizing the prisoner, resulted in a complete regression when the human being became unable to separate once more the inner from the outer worlds. Some reached a point of insanity when they could no longer distinguish the real from the unreal. In this 'somnabulant' state of near-hypnosis one obeyed orders without question, endured pain often without being aware of it, and was capable of performing exhausting work for fourteen to sixteen hours a day for weeks and months on end.

I remember this state of mind only too well, and it is this, more than anything I have witnessed in the outer world, that still fills me with horror. It is this area of *feeling* that most concentration camp graduates are reluctant to talk about, though they may talk freely about the horrible conditions and other external factors they have seen. Many, however, forget this infantile state of mind, just as we forget the infantile experiences of our beginnings, and probably for the same reasons.

I was affected in this way during the summer of 1944 in the camp of Troglitz in Thuringia. The temporary insanity (I cannot call it anything else, although it was not insanity in the civilized sense) lasted about six weeks, after which, through an attempted escape, I managed to regain some contact with reality.

This peculiar state of mind did not attack me suddenly, but developed gradually. It started with enuresis. Night after night I woke to find that I had wetted myself, so I had to sleep in a lower bunk, a place coveted by my comrades for the same reason. I often felt during those days that I was also going to soil myself, but I always managed to reach the latrine in time. Others, however, were not so fortunate. In fact, the majority of people in the camp of Troglitz were unable to control themselves in this way. It was something that filled us with horror and shame, and we denied it if caught in the act. Although a man might have soiled himself that very night, if he caught another doing the same, he became abusive and aggressive. I remember my history master, a man in his late fifties, wetting himself one night and being caught by an ex-architect, who attacked him both physically and verbally. The culprit, far from defending himself, started to cry, repeating : 'I promise you it will never happen again, I promise you, I promise you, forgive me. . . .' Later that night the tables were turned on the architect and a very similar scene occurred between him and someone else.

Usually at night I found myself sucking my left thumb, with saliva smeared all over my face. Sometimes I had beautiful dreams of trees and flowers and sunshine; I remember vividly a dream of two trees, inclined like a V sign, and between the two a huge red rose that trembled in the wind. Then there were times when I dreamed that I was running, tired, breathless, perspiring, through endless fields that had no beginning and no end. Sometimes these dreams spilled over into the translucent greyness of the day, until it was impossible to tell which was reality and which illusion. I began to view myself as if I were not myself at all, but someone quite different, as though I were at home, sitting comfortably in an armchair, watching the scenes of some film of which I myself was the hero being projected before my own eyes.

Although at times I had vivid sexual dreams, desire took second place. My mother became a Goddess in my mind, and I began to pray to her for help. I don't remember any stage of my life when I felt nearer to her than in Troglitz. My father and sister never entered my thoughts until just before the liberation. I lived in a state of blissful union with my mother, talking to her, sometimes aloud, as if it was a real conversation. Sometimes I almost heard her voice talking to me. I could not have survived the camps without this 'contact'.

Under such circumstances aggression was turned against the

self. Suicide, or suicidal acts (like running away from an S.S. man who had ordered the prisoner to report to him, or 'falling' against an electrified fence) were not uncommon. We recognized our weaknesses, of course, more in others than in ourselves. If one wanted to survive, one could not tolerate the pessimists who foretold death. One sought the company of the dreamers, those who saw the 'signs'. Anyone who was destined to survive had to believe in the possibility of a miracle.

Indeed, we not only 'regressed' into our personal childhood, but in some sense collectively into the universal childhood of Mankind. There are some indications that the Homo Auschwitziensis was a modern 're-incarnation' of the Homo Heidelbergiensis. With the loss of culture, the framework of an established social order and modern civilization, Man regressed into the period of pre-history, before the dawn of civilized existence. Had the concentration camps lasted much longer, cannibalism would have become an everyday phenomenon. The meaning of Society has a special significance to those who survived the camps. The social order that we have created throughout the millenia maintains Man as Man. If this order were to be lost through a new atomic war, the whole of remaining Mankind would have to start afresh, for Mankind would go back to the jungle.

The concentration camps could be divided into two main groups : camps where the internal power was concentrated in the hands of previously anti-social groups, such as criminals; and those where political prisoners had the opportunity of administration. I suffered four camps : Auschwitz, Buchenwald, Troglitz and Berga-Elster. In Auschwitz and Troglitz the camp was in the hands of the criminals; in Buchenwald and Berga-Elster in the hands of the politicals. In Auschwitz and Troglitz prisoners lost all their humanity; in Buchenwald and Berga-Elster they did not.

How it happened that this or that group managed to get hold of the internal administration of a camp is a complicated story. Each camp, as far as the S.S. was concerned, had its own purpose. There were camps where the sole purpose of the S.S. was to annihilate people; such a camp was Auschwitz-Birkenau and Troglitz. Then there were others where their purpose was to use the prisoners to work for the Reich, as in Buchenwald, and also Berga-Elster. But whatever the purpose of the S.S., this was also changed according to Himmler's instructions. Buchenwald started off as an extermination camp, and later became a 'work-camp'. Auschwitz was in time split into two camps; Birkenau started and remained to the end an extermination camp; and Auschwitz proper was a work-camp.

In the extermination camps the S.S. wanted chaos to reign; in the work camps it was in their interest to have some order. They found that political prisoners, particularly the communists, could organize camp life much better than criminals. In Buchenwald, for example, the politicals openly resented the rule of the criminals and were eventually given key positions.

What a close relationship there is between Society and Man's emotions I learned while in Germany. Auschwitz and Troglitz created and maintained a 'jungle society'; Buchenwald and Berga-Elster created a society where the regressive forces operated to a lesser degree, and where once more one could feel proud to be a human being.

The 'Politicals' *knew* why they were in the camps, and most of them had not forgotten that they had a purpose in life : the destruction of National Socialism. In the camps they could do no more than demonstrate that through comradeship some law and order could be maintained. The condition for this, of course, lay in the fact that they had the key-positions i.e. the administration of the kitchen, distribution of food, running of prison 'Reviers' (so called Hospitals) etc. They were also in charge of barracks and work-groups. As well as the shared hatred directed against the common enemy, they also held in common an un-

failing belief in a better future life. While it is true to say that
the Communists held the leading positions in Buchenwald, there
were of course other political prisoners there too; social demo-
crats, clericals and other 'enemies of the Reich'.

It is also true that for some time the various political groups
regarded each other with some hostility, but as time went on the
spirit of comradeship was extended to all. In Buchenwald there
was less thieving of food than in the 'non-political' camps, and
the general attitude of prisoners to each other was based on
tolerance and understanding. In this kind of camp one could
find friends, and discuss things in a much more adult fashion;
through comradeship one could 'belong' once more. This feeling
of belonging gave most of us a new internal strength.

There was a clearly defined hierarchy in Buchenwald. The
'Politicals', particularly the Communists, represented the
aristocracy. They wore excellent clothing, had enough to eat
(everybody was equal in Buchenwald, but some were a little
more equal than others), had 'good jobs', and were usually 'old'
prisoners.

Following the Communists came the other politicals who also
had quite decent clothing, but were not as spotless as the Communists. They also had jobs which did not involve much manual
labour. The 'old' criminals, conscientious objectors, Jehovah's
Witnesses, homosexuals (i.e. those who had been convicted of
that 'crime'), represented the middle classes. The non-political
Jew belonged to the proletariat.

During the first part of my imprisonment I belonged to the
unprivileged class as merely one of millions, but from December
1944 I suddenly became a member of the aristocracy. One's
outlook changed according to one's position in camp life. The
emotional reaction of the prisoner belonging to the lower strata
was not at all the same as that of one belonging to the upper
strata.

A Danish prisoner, Niels Ahlmark, a policeman from Copenhagen (who survived the camp and subsequently returned to his duties in the Police force in his country), helped me from his Red Cross parcels to get extra nourishment, so that in time I put on weight and my physical appearance more nearly resembled that of the 'rulers'. He also gave me a brand new suit of Danish military uniform, and never in my life have I looked so impressive as I did in Buchenwald. When I was transferred to another camp (Berga-Elster) my appearance among other things helped me to become a 'Vorarbeiter' (foreman) in the camp kitchen, one of the most coveted posts in the camp. I thus overnight became one of the leaders.

I have described how I felt in Troglitz, and that description would perhaps be representative of the feelings of the masses in the extermination camps. Now that I had managed to break free from such mass existence, I found myself feeling differently, acting differently, and, of course, eating differently.

The opposite to regression is freedom : freedom of thought, and speech, freedom of action, freedom of movement. In the work camps of Buchenwald and Berga-Elster I regained some of these freedoms, except of course the freedom of movement— though even this was greater than before, because I could move freely within the camp (unlike Auschwitz or Troglitz). It seemed that it was absolutely essential to express as many of these freedoms as possible to maintain my sanity. The freedom to express thought is an indication that one is not entirely at the mercy of internal and external forces; it enables one to face the darkness and the enemy. When I could say to my comrades : 'These bastards will one day disappear from the face of the earth', it meant to me that this was indeed a possibility. How very important this human communication was to me and to others, I had never considered before I entered the camps; but there I came to the conclusion that one of the greatest things in life is the ability to speak, to listen, to communicate, to agree, to disagree, to feel. To quote a few lines of a poem to a fellow-prisoner meant to both of us that a world of poetry really existed, *because* it

existed in us. No German could destroy the work of Heine because it was spoken in the heart.

Freedom of action, particularly forbidden action, was also of
great importance. Now that fate had given me an opportunity
to *do* something positive I had to use my leading position to
translate this into reality. There was an American camp nearby,
and soldiers from it came to collect the 'Ersatz coffee' every
morning. I decided to persuade my comrades to fill the jugs with
boiled potatoes. Not only did I do this because I genuinely
wanted to help my American comrades, but because an act of
danger in defiance of the S.S. was one more reminder that I was
not entirely in their power. By helping others, I also helped
myself. There were a great number of Russian prisoners of war
in Berga-Elster, who were particularly badly treated by the S.S.
We in the kitchen decided to supply some of them with boiled
potatoes too. It was a risky undertaking, but each success was a
personal victory over the enemy.

It was through these exchanges and episodes that I gradually
developed a new meaning for my own life, and for Life itself.
It was as if I had managed to penetrate some mystery hitherto
not fully understood. It represents to this very day the founda-
tion of a particular brand of faith.

The world now considers concentration camps as belonging
to the past. Some, in fact, have become 'museums', where
qualified guides now conduct the visitor round the remains of
the gas chambers and the crematoria. Today you may take a
coach-tour from Weimar to Buchenwald, or from Crakow to
Auschwitz. You may eat your sandwiches and chew your
chewing-gum while being shown round, and when tired you
can sit on the benches put up for your comfort and thank God
that the past is dead. But is it?

There are thousands of men and women all over the world to
whom that past is never dead. The survivors of concentration
camps have regained their old names, and their old prison

number is only a memory; yet there is hardly a day when a dream, a sudden fear, an anxious moment or a sharp physical pain does not remind us that within the dark layers of our minds time stands still.

The outer world is connected with the inner, the invisible wires send messages to and fro. Bloodshed in the Congo, the murder of whites and blacks, the agony of starving millions, trigger off in us a desperate fear for our own lives and that of humanity. The bombs exploding in the atmosphere carry a message of such vast hopelessness into our inner world, that at times we have to use every ounce of our strength not to give up life and to go on as before. We cannot tolerate intolerance, we cannot stand prejudice, and yet tragically we who have remained are the most prejudiced of all.

I used to speak German quite fluently, for it was my second tongue; I was taught by a Fraulein from Bavaria when I was small. During the war I spoke German with hardly any accent, and yet today I cannot utter a German sentence. I had to go to Düsseldorf some years ago to be present when my German compensation claim was being considered. I arrived at the airport and wanted to order a taxi, but I could only utter English words. I tried my hardest at the interview to speak German. It was a complete failure. I understood every word the German said, but I could not speak German to him.

Apart from the language barrier there are other barriers too. Last summer in Italy some young Germans joined my table at the hotel, and something in me froze so that I felt literally sick, and had to leave them. It was no use telling myself that this was a new generation who had nothing to do with Hitler and the concentration camps; a terrible voice repeated within me that they are a cursed race, and collectively guilty for the past. How can I, of all people, talk of a 'cursed race', when this was *their* own evil argument? It seems as if I have been infected by *them*, and cannot shake off the disease however much in common sense I may wish to do so. I seem to carry my enemy within myself.

The other day the B.B.C. Television screened 'Oliver Twist', and when I saw the portrayl of Fagin, that evil man, whose every appearance was accompanied by a picture of the Star of David, I was paralysed. I felt as if the B.B.C. was involved in some major conspiracy against my people and for several nights I slept badly.

Today I am a Psychiatric Social Worker, and in my professional capacity I come across people who were inmates of those camps. There is little doubt in my mind that the many breakdowns that occur in them are the direct result of the terrible experiences they went through.

Where concentration camp imprisonment coincided with the pre-adolescent period, the emotional scars received are most apparent in terms of difficult inter-personal relationships, particularly in marriage. I found that this was a subject that most concentration camp victims wanted to hide from the German Authorities in connection with their compensation claims. In these individuals there seems to be an almost complete split between emotional and sexual functioning; as the emotions have been arrested before the adolescent phase, most of them seek their salvation through sex. Their sexual appetite is the greater because they are unable to satisfy some other inner need. In fact, sexual promiscuity among former inmates of camps is high, but they are invariably unhappy and unsatisfied people. There are few broken marriages, though, because they are frightened to break up any relationship. This is a serious problem, and only a very few dare to seek help by consulting some specialist. The majority carry on before an unsuspecting world.

*   *   *

But there is another side to the coin. Those of us who were caught up in the Nazi web *after* our adolescence, when our emotional pattern was already formed, have learned something in the camp that no other form of education could have given us. We have learnt the value of freedom and of Life itself. It was in Buchenwald that I learned from Jews, Christians, Moslems and pagans, from Englishmen, Serbs, Rumanians, Czechs, Frenchmen, Belgians, Dutch, Russians, Greeks, Albanians, Poles and Italians that I was only one more suffering insignificant man; that the tongue my mother taught me, and my Hungarian memories, and the traditions of my nation, were nothing but artificial barriers between myself and others. For essentially, as Mankind, we are one. A slap on the face hurts an Englishman as much as it does a German, Hungarian or Negro. The pain is the same; only our attitude to the pain differs, according to the culture-pattern of the country and the individual. Our dreams, each dreamt in a different language, spell out the same dream in the language of Mankind; all of us want peace, security, a life free from fear. And, each in his own way, irrespective of differences of nationality or race, we seek for the meaning or meaningless of life and death, believe in God or deny Him, cry for a woman on whose bosom we may rest our tormented head. I also learned that it is a fallacy that there are great nations and little nations : there are merely nations which occupy a large territory, and others which have less land. Greatness and smallness can exist side by side in any nation, just as they do in the case of individuals. This in its turn taught me to understand the pointlessness of ambition for the sake of fame or success, because as I was I was neither worse nor better than others. During the long walks with my comrades I learnt to understand that within me, as in others, the murderer and the humanitarian exist side by side; the weak child with the voracious male. That I am not in any way superior, that I am not different from others, that I am but a link in the great chain, was amongst the greatest discoveries of my life. From then on I resolved to support those who fell, even as I had been supported. When someone was despicable, greedy and selfish, I remembered all the occasions when I too, had been despicable, greedy and selfish. Buchenwald taught me to be tolerant of myself, and by that means tolerant of others.

ASSISTED BY THUGS

By Paul Ignotus

LOOKING back over the period of more than six and a half years spent in prison, I have often tried to sum up what it was like. Surely each day was not the same? I can remember clearly the first forty-eight hours and fairly clearly the last twenty-four. A score of days and some hundreds of moments, for reasons known or unknown to me, stand out; but memory can only recall these isolated events, not the flow of time. The more truthful one is determined to be in describing what prison was like, the more one has to generalize and conjecture. One cannot rely on facts alone, where these are too numerous to mention in one breath. A philosopher, treading in Eleatic footsteps, may question whether that flow of happenings was reality at all : was it not, to an even greater degree than the path of the arrow through the air, divided and subdivided into an infinity of microcosmic particles lacking any logical connection with each other and only united through the wilful dreams of our minds?

The answer to the metaphysical part of this question is obvious : if you doubt the reality of imprisonment, try it and then give your opinion.

This is good advice and has often been followed by excellent brains in the face of comparable problems. Molière's hero thrashed the philosopher who doubted the reality of man's existence : why should he cry out if he knew the blows were illusory?

Dr. Johnson solved the problem even more laconically by kicking a stone to provide the proof sought for its existence and movability. This method might indeed be adequate to dispense with theoretical difficulties about whether a stick is a stick or a stone a stone; whether a sensation reflects an objective entity or whether something set moving does indeed move : but I did try prison and neither while I was trying it, nor now looking back on it, can I believe that it was a reality.

My incredulity may in fact have been one of my reasons for trying it. It was not the only one and certainly not the most influential. I vividly recall the qualms I had, when as Hungarian Press Counsellor in London in May, 1949, I decided to obey the order of the Government Department summoning me to Budapest. I knew the journey would be full of risks : being hanged or tortured to death were only two of the possibilities I reckoned with. After some heart-searching, I gave myself two reasons for deciding to accept the invitation : the first concerned principles; the second—personal ties.

Though I was a sceptic, I always took principles seriously. I did not mind ridiculing them but my own laughter was not allowed to deter me from standing up for what I knew to be right : *ex officio scriptoris,* I felt this to be my job. My concern to bridge the widening gulf between Britain, then under a Labour Government, and Hungary, not yet completely Stalinist, was strengthened both by these principles and by the alarming developments of 1949. I was as sincere in my attempt as I was doubtful. However hopeless the task seemed, my disgust with those English and Hungarian gentry who *wanted* it to be hopeless was enough to prevent me giving up. My passion for the left was undiluted; in a way it is so today.

But I have always been suspicious of my own motives and I suspected even then that this concern or passion of mine would have taken an entirely different course, if it had not been for my personal ties with people who were at the mercy of the Stalinist authorities. I had parents and a brother and sister in Budapest as well as other relatives and close friends. I went on hoping against hope that, if I stayed in my job, either the situation at home would improve or else that I would somehow be able to help them and eventually they would be able to leave the country and settle in England. Was I fooling myself? Certainly, I knew I was, but I felt that if I did not fool myself in this way, I could not avoid fooling myself in an even more irritating way. For what was the alternative; to resign from my job and seek refuge in Britain? Yes, I argued, this may be the sounder course and it would be not only safer for me but it may also ultimately benefit those I am so anxious not to harm. If I remain in London and the situation does not deteriorate too rapidly in Budapest, I might be able to help them, whereas if things become hopeless over there, at least I should feel that there was nothing I could have done.

I rejected these arguments, convinced that such palliatives could not work for me. Perhaps the arrest or internment and maltreatment of people attached to me would occur quite irrespective of my actions, but I knew that I would never be satisfied that it had not been caused by my staying abroad. My own subsequent security would become a nightmare to me, and the more eloquently I proved to myself that I could have done nothing, the more I would be afraid that I was deceiving myself. It was that fear that I wished to escape from when I chose the dangerous course. 'I lacked the courage to be a coward,' I later complained in a prison poem.

The danger had its appeal. Though I had gone through a great deal, including being harassed by the authorities, I had never tasted imprisonment proper. So many of my friends had experienced it, some escaping death by the skin of their teeth in Auschwitz; others held up for just ten hours in a shack by a frontier guard until they were cleared, with apologies. . . . These very different sorts of imprisonment concerned adult people, who, while they lasted, had to get special permission to leave a room. This degrading situation struck me as too fantastic to be real. How would I face up to something like that? What would it be like and, more important, what would I be like afterwards? There was a challenging test of endurance concealed in the grim possibilities threatening me.

The challenge came. I kept repeating how unbelievable it was while I was experiencing it; but the opposite is also true; it was not only believable but it was unbelievable that it could ever have been different. There I lay on what served as my bed—bed or wooden bunk or half a straw sack, varying according to the orders of the Political Police who acted as our Destiny—there I lay at dawn with my limbs stiffened by ingrained discomfort and defence against the cold, slowly preparing to open my eyes to the familiar rhythm of banging doors and rattling pails, to another day about to start. Soon the gaoler, a piece of sub-human omnipotence in uniform, would be coming round; the bed would be made, the cell swept and the black luke-warm liquid poured into dixies. Still chewing our bread, we would hear another round of banging doors and catch the whiffs of fresh air and fermented urine; then it would be the line-up for exercises. It all seemed so deadly natural, so unalterable and pre-destined. Could it ever have been different? Could I ever have been in a position simply to open a door and go for a walk and then to return home and relax as I felt like, with or without a *casual* friend.

Casual: this is the operative word. The joy of being able to choose the inessential seemed then a Kingdom Come, a kingdom gone, one that had never existed. 'Now that you have gone through all those things, what would you say was essential in life?' a friend asked me after my release. He was a poet, even a good one, usually unrhetorical, with a gift for suddenly exploding great commonplaces. We were sitting in the mild breeze and sunshine, in modest luxury on the terrace of a Budapest bistro, between two meetings. 'Essential?' I answered, 'the essential is to be able to loiter over a glass of beer in the sun and breeze and stretch yourself quietly when you are ready to leave.' He gave me a stern look : 'That's not enough.' Of course this was true, but even if I had known it theoretically before, I should have learned from experience in prison, that the main consolation for the course of human destiny is the stream of liberties too trifling to be noticed and too trivial to be proclaimed.

*   *   *

What would it be like to be beaten up? Again, my fear of it did not prevent me from wishing to experience it. It was silly, of course, as, even more than in the case of imprisonment, I could surmise what it would be like from details with which I had been only too familiar. I had fought a lot as a schoolboy and even when middle-aged had got involved in brawls with the Nazis. Besides, I had been maltreated physically as well as mentally from the moment of my arrest onwards, so that when I learned that I was to be given a 'proper hiding', I might have known that the difference would be one of ritual, or at the most of degree, rather than of kind. Yet I was still curious to know how I would stand it, not merely the physical pain but the fantastic situation of being an adult person, a so-called gentleman, who, when attacked with fists and truncheons, was not supposed to hit back.

Here, the words *supposed to* are crucial. They have perhaps an additional interpretation for one brought up like myself in a country with the morality of duels and 'affairs of honour' still alive. In the Hungary of my youth, to get one's ears boxed was a symbol; 'the slap in the face' was an institution. The sharper the clack and the design of the four fingers on the cheek, the more significant its meaning. If it was handed out by a bailiff to a farmhand, it was just a paternalistic reprimand. If given by a lady to an over-forward young man it was expected to be taken with good nature; if the youth was smart he would smile, click his heels and rejoin, 'Oh, I adore you when you lose your temper'. But one gentleman slapping another, giving him a *pofon,* as a proper slap on the cheek is called, was an action asking for murder if not for *harakiri.*

Surely my country was not the only one where such reactions were usual? The expression 'a slap in the face' has an allegorical meaning attached to it in practically every language. But there are different degrees of seriousness in interpreting that meaning. My country, and my native town, Budapest, a sharp-witted, jocular and in many ways sophisticated city, was as solemn, stupid and humourless as it could be about this question. How many tragedies and how much malicious gossip arose over a few *pofons*! 'Mind you, he got a *pofon* from . . . and now you see them arm-in-arm. What a cad,' a whisper would go round. 'But, then, he did hit back, didn't he, and they did have a duel,' the meek defence ran. 'I should jolly well think so,' came the reply, with a sardonic grin. His hitting back had not succeeded as a pofon, not a real one as no one had heard its *clap* and no one had been killed or even seriously injured in that duel. The wretched 'cad' had of course made an attempt to keep up gentlemanly appearances, but just you know . . . the triumphant and malignant giggles spread and he was done for.

There is no need to say that the leftish intelligentsia to which I belonged despised this attitude, but it was as helpless in sharing it as were the Popular Front Etonians in repressing a shudder at the comrade who dropped his aitches in political discussion. Conventions are stronger than the rational objections to them, and the humiliation of a so-called gentleman, deprived of the power to retaliate when being hit, was something beyond my powers of imagination.

So-called is here the operative word for there were borderline cases of gentlemanliness; as, for instance, in the schoolmaster of Jewish origin who had taken part in the underground Communist movement. He was beaten up by the political police, 'just like a navvy', and served six months in prison. He later became a writer and one evening as we called in to a bar for a glass of *fröcs* (wine and soda), he nudged me and pointed to a hefty looking figure. It was the notorious detective inspector who, with his squad, had tortured my friend and many others. 'What does it feel like to meet him now,' I asked, 'in this no-man's land, as it were, remembering what he did to you?' My companion did not answer. He did not seem embarrassed but frowned as if he simply didn't know.

I had a writer friend who came from a peasant family and who had been beaten up several times at the beginning of his literary career by the police, not so much for his inflammatory ideas, which they didn't understand anyway, but for the fact that, though only a poor plotholder, he had dared to poke his nose into those printed incomprehensibilities with which it was the gentlemen's prerogative to deal. Later he was discovered, and owing to the political fashion of those years, he acquired the social privileges of white-collared respectability or, at least, of its bohemian fringes and was no longer beaten up when caught reading or writing. 'But do you still see those men who beat you up every day in the street?' I asked. My friend admitted that he did. 'What does it feel like now to see those men whose blows you had to put up with without being able to retaliate?' I continued. My friend, being a protagonist of rural simplicity, answered in dynamic and extremely involved sentences about the tasks of the *gendarmerie,* the utility and futility of the co-operative movement among the peasantry, the blessings and evils of tribal heritage, the differences between Altaic and Semitic and Aryan racial instincts, and the prospects for combining dialectical materialism with the creed of Blood and Soil. 'All this sounds fascinating,' I kept repeating, 'but *what does it feel like?*' This friend, with all his eloquence provided no more of an answer than did the other in his reticence. The former school-teacher simply did not know; the former peasant simply did not understand.

Now, some twelve years later, I tested myself. I am not concerned here with the physical suffering involved, but with the feeling of helplessness in the face of the aggressors. The moment of testing my reactions did not come at the time of my 'proper hiding' but later. After my uneasy and unequal pact with the political police about the lies I was to 'confess' to had been concluded and I had been granted six cigarettes a day in my underground cell, I was allowed, like the others in my position, to ask the gaoler for a light while he was inspecting me through the peep-hole. The chief inspector of the cells was also the chief of the beating up squad—a swollen-faced man, proficient, I imagine, at all kinds of tortures, and who as a 'jolly good fellow' liked to amuse his helpers. I did not have to wait long until I saw his eye through the hole. 'Well, now I will see what it *feels* like,' I told myself, and holding a cigarette I hurried to the door, 'Chief Inspector, sir, would you be so very kind as to give me a light?' My voice did not tremble and it did not feel like anything. To get a light from him was no more of a sensation than to get a box of matches out of a slot-machine.

How wise my friends had been not to know the answer to my question. How intelligent they had been not even to understand it. Surely the experience did not teach me anything that I had not known before, anything about morals, I mean. When arguing about questions like this I had always quoted Schopenhauer's contemptuous remarks about the gentry who thought that if they were kicked by a beast, they must risk their life in a ritual fight with it or else they could no longer be regarded as *chevaleresques*. Now I was faced by the beast-man; beast if ever there was one, more so than actually wicked or devilish. Did I *feel* as I stood by the door that he was only a beast? Not even that; I felt, if anything, that he was a brick that had fallen on my head and that could now be used as a slot-machine. 'Thank you, Chief Inspector, sir,' I said after a puff and congratulated myself for having got rid of a nightmare.

*   *   *

In this way prison taught me to be humble. It also taught me to be arrogant. These teachings do not conflict; in a way they are complementary. Could I continue to consider myself a man of honour after I had received a *pofon* and had felt no more than physically affronted? I found that I no longer cared about the whole question. Whether through saintliness or moral apathy, I had at any rate rid myself of this form of snobbishness.

This does not mean that I did not experience snobbery in prison. On the contrary, I saw a dazzling kaleidoscope of its varieties. It was pathetic, amusing and paradoxical. After all, snobbery cannot survive without accepted social values. Even its most sophisticated and intellectual brands imply a tribute to a social type worthy of imitation, reverence or associating with. We political prisoners under Stalin's rule were a society of frieze-dressed cripples, caricatures of the social values which had dwindled and collapsed before and during our imprisonment. We dragged ourselves along in our sweat-soaked, ill-fitting uniforms, with our bristly, emaciated faces, often trembling in the hope of an extra dixie-full of the foul food. There we were, counts and bishops, ci-devants of all classes and denominations, former generals of the Nazi machine which set out to conquer the world, former generals of the resistance against the Nazi machine, former officers of the political police holding us under its thumb; a whole universe of smartness and counter-smartness, now ragged, stinking and miserable. Were we impressed with ourselves, with our former social standing, wealth and brilliance? Or were we impressed by our masters, the new top-dogs? They struck us all as being far coarser, clumsier and more ludicrous in their omnipotence than anything we had ever seen or imagined. We had only contempt for them, laughing at their pompous solecisms and shuddering with disgust at their crudeness and cruelty. Which should have attracted us then, the wrecks of past glory or the set of thugs laboriously attempting to shine in their stead? The new type of success seemed as absurd as any of the former manifestations. Nevertheless, both sorts proved themselves attractive to prisoners, who irrespective of their political leanings and backgrounds, fell prey to social fascination. Their attitudes to Power and Glory cut across Party lines.

There were the believers in armed authority, often its professional and devoted tools. Many of them came from the *gendarmerie* or the *Gestapo* or the Red or White political police. It was a foregone conclusion that they would be nostalgic for their former glory and proud of what they used to stand for and also that they would be eager to act as the right-hand men of their present gaolers. However, this characteristic is too crude to be listed as snobbery although it may border on it. It should really be treated, without moral prejudice, under the heading 'Gangsterism as a Pillar of Social Order'. Some careful research might demonstrate that no régime has yet emerged which has been able to dispense with this Pillar altogether, although, no doubt, Right and Left-wing totalitarian dictatorships make fuller use of it than any other form of government.

A far gentler group than these were the old noblemen of the former privileged upper-middle classes, the near-aristocrats now in sad decay. There were, for instance, the two old companions lying side by side in the prison hospital, who were addressed by everyone, in the compulsory intimacy of our misery, as Uncle Andor and Uncle Laci. When, at one time, I joined them in the ward, I found that for about ten days they had hardly been on speaking terms. 'What's wrong with old Laci?' I asked Uncle Andor, who was more than just a comrade-in-frieze of mine; he considered himself, not quite unreasonably, as my comrade in isolation. He was a doctor by profession and a fairly highly reputed scientist who had travelled a great deal in the West making friends with American colleagues and diplomatists and so precipitating his own downfall under the Stalin régime. He also displayed a quite encyclopaedic if somewhat whimsical interest in subjects ranging from Shakespeare and Orwell to trout-fishing and Free-Masonry. 'You know what a narrow-minded, ignorant fool Laci is,' he began. I certainly did, but on the other hand I really liked old Laci, rather as a joke of a man. He had been an aide-de camp to Regent Horthy and had a reputation of being an excellent horseman, a complete illiterate and a jolly-good chap. Now half-dead in prison he lived up to his reputation, entertaining the nurses with time-honoured dirty stories whenever he had the chance and making no effort to conceal the simple mind which had so endeared him to the ex-Regent, who considered him the embodiment of reliable, Christian and gentlemanly patriotism. Obviously Uncle Andor could not see eye-to-eye with him on every point but then why discuss anything with him at all? 'For heaven's sake, Uncle Andor,' I said, 'let him die in peace as he is : I hope you are not trying to convert him to liberalism after his long years in brilliant uniform and now in prison. . . .' Uncle Andor shook his head, 'It's nothing to do with liberalism,' he said, 'but you know how he likes to be referred to as "the old *hussar*". Even the nurse sergeant pats him on the back and shouts, "Still here, not in bloody hell yet, you old hussar", and he beams with pleasure. I said to him, "Look here Laci, you know you've never been a hussar; you served with the mounted artillery until Horthy made you a brigadier, so I don't call *that* a hussar"! Now, can you imagine what a temper he got into? He went red and shouted, "You spoil everything, you can't tell me what I have been, I know better than you, it's none of your business", and so on. Fancy *him* trying to fool *me*. Not that I care anyway, but *I* served with the hussars in my National Service, so he can't get away with. . . .'

In the end it was Uncle Andor who died first, still unreconciled. Uncle Laci carried on, dragging his limbs round and muttering his jokes. When the smell of the Thaw reached us from outside, he was full of hopes for an early release. He was encouraged by the fact that discrimination against the descendants of the former ruling classes had recently become less 'dogmatic' and that in consequence one of his nephews had been awarded an efficiency prize in a factory. 'Mind you,' he said with apparent satisfaction, 'the deputy Minister himself pinned the medal on his lapel; and a very beautiful medal it was.' No matter who the masters are, Honour is honour.

*   *   *

No less conspicuous than the self-abasement of the haughty *ci-devants* towards the upstart overlords was the fascination with past splendour noticeable among the plebeians, and irrespective of their social backgrounds among the avowed revolutionaries. The awe with which they gazed at our fellow prisoner, Prince Esterhazy, the top magnate of ancient Hungary, whatever their professed opinions, gave them away. The magnetism of family trees, real or invented, was tremendous. Many prisoners boasted about their noble ancestry; others, in conformity with the class-racialism enacted by the Stalinists, bragged of their 'proletarian' pedigree; quite a few succeeded in combining the two. For Jews, the obvious course was to ponder on their own ordeal, in the light of what their people had gone through, and to take some melancholy pride in belonging to the most ancient aristocracy of the persecuted, the race chosen to suffer. But what was more striking was that, in conditions like these, the virulence of what Theodore Lessing has called *jüdischer Selbsthass* persisted with the painful dissimulation of *les Juifs honteux*.

After the air-raids, as many English readers will remember, one of the weirdest sights was to find among the ruins some raw eggs or dainty sherry glasses that had survived the blast without a crack. I found it equally strange to see how psychical complexes remained unaffected by social upheavals. There was, it is true, certain practical reasons for obscuring one's Jewish background; in some of the prison industrial plants, such as the 'Gamma' lighter factory, Nazi convicts were allowed to enforce their own racial laws for the sake of efficient teamwork; the gaolers, many of them subconscious or even near-conscious Nazis, were encouraged by their officers, often *Juifs honteux* themselves, to indulge in raids on 'Zionist' prisoners. But this did not altogether account for the neurosis of shamefaced Jewishness which I witnessed.

This seemed to be most grotesque and heartrending when indoctrinated communists were its victims. There was a former journalist who had served as an officer in the International Brigade in Spain; this fact alone made his snobbish inhibitions seem even more puzzling. He liked to pose as a man of humble but thoroughbred Hungarian stock. Those who shared his cell were struck by his habit of dangling a shirt in front of him as he sat on the lavatory or of hastily turning his face to the wall as he stood under the shower. Had he been shy about sex and bodily matters in general, this would not have been surprising, but on the contrary, a rude noise was for him a tremendous joke. He was merely terrified it would be discovered that he had been circumcized.[1] He made violently anti-Semitic statements wherever these could be fitted into Party jargon : the Jewish capitalists were the greediest exploiters and the Zionists were the most cruel race-exterminators the world had ever seen. Some of his cellmates would lose patience and become rude : 'We know you are a Jew yourself, and what gymnastics you perform to hide your. . . .' He would nervously bite his soldierly moustache and continue with his 'gymnastics'. What a hell his life must have been. A special hell within the communal hell. However, he was not dogmatic and knew the family tree of the Rothschilds as well as a gossip columnist; as a good Stalinist, a peerage impressed him even if it decorated a Jew. Proletarian class-consciousness has no effect at all on social snobbery and its psycho-pathological corollaries.

*   *   *

Men at liberty live side by side, shrouded by clouds of deceit. Are these clouds removed by bodily proximity? Not in my ex-

---

[1] In Central Europe, circumcision for prophilactic hygiene is practically unknown; it is still the sign—or the stigma—of the Covenant.

perience. Men don't stop deceiving each other because they are sharing the same strawsack. Even between two snores, they go on lying in their gestures and accents. Stewed in one and the same saucepan, they go out of their way to impress their fellow victims.

Intellectual snobbery too, was rampant, mainly in its most adolescent varieties : the attempt to outstrip one another in knowing the names of past and present-day celebrities, in speaking foreign languages fluently, in having read widely or at least in pretending to have done so. It was usual, especially in the long periods of enforced idleness, to play parlour games; one of these consisted in choosing any letter of the alphabet and then seeing who could think of the greatest number of famous personalities whose names began with that letter. No doubt, it was a good pastime, but how unnatural and even tragic were the vanities vested in it. People blushed for not knowing a name that others did or for being hoaxed into pretending to know one that had never existed. I can recall hysterical scenes where points of honour were raised about names rightly or wrongly remembered. A cellmate, whose pride had been hurt would pace the six feet at his disposal in grim taciturnity, or deliver an address of florid and rhetorical self-assertion while squatting over the sanitary bucket. There is, I felt, no such thing as nakedness of the mind : there is only exhibitionism which is usually more attitudinizing than conventional formalities. Men cannot live without lies, certainly not in slavery.

When did *others* catch *me* lying, I wonder. I never caught them catching me, but then I never caught myself. I am not speaking of lies told for convenience; everyone, including myself, would indulge in those, though I have always found it more comfortable not to, except where the basic rules of tact require it. What I really mean is, was there any deception in my attitude; was I acting? The answer is, not that I know of. Therefore I am bound to believe that either I am a person of exceptional intellectual honesty, such as I have hardly ever encountered, or else

that my self-deceptions are buried so deeply that not even the
long years spent face to face with my own sweating carcass, with
the evidence of my companions' lies in front of me, could bring
them to the surface. Either—or? My guess is that there might
be some truth in both these assumptions. Suffering did not
estrange me from my rational opinions but helped me to break
down the gap between them and myself. I had never thought it
a disgrace to get a *pofon;* prison taught me to feel as I thought.
I always knew that sincerity was a rare gift and prison taught me
to take its shrill disguises for granted. The Universe consists of
motes and in prison I learned to see them in every eye. I still
have not discovered the beam in mine.

*   *   *

Have I not? Of course I have and I am carrying it along in
the shape of cosmic guilt; this, if anything, excuses my self-
contentment. I would not dare to confess to my conceit unless
I knew it to be a fake. Every soul, human or non-human, is an
edifice of lies and I cannot be an exception. My edifice has a
facade of modesty; it has walls of superiority behind it but these
are built, again, on foundations of modesty—metaphysical
modesty, I should say, a feeling of nothingness, an overwhelming
impression of being in the world due to some unaccountable mistake that has to be atoned for. This feeling is not confined to
prison but it does develop in that environment where cries coming *de profundis* have a dramatic setting and where vague hopes
for outside help may crystallize into a belief in God. The un-
believer may not come across any evidence to modify his
disbelief, but even so he may, as in my case, become more and
more sympathetic towards those who do.

Strangely enough I even found myself in sympathy with
ostentatious believers, of whom Tolstoy was the greatest. Ironically, it was due to the cult of 'everything Russian', aimed at

promoting communist internationalism as devised by the Krem-
lin, that I was able to obtain nearly all Tolstoy's works in
Hungarian translation from the prison library. The first thing
that struck me about his writing was his familiarity with prison
experience.

A prisoner's mind becomes obsessed by prison. He is continually affronted by the fact that people outside can carry on with
their ordinary lives without being affected by the ordeal he and
his companions are undergoing. He may find a story beautiful
or a play interesting but he is constantly asking himself why an
author does not write about '*them*'. How can a plot be conceived
without reference to the dangers, privations, and suffering as
exemplified by prison life? I realized this was a silly question but
I could not help asking it again and again. I felt that as a
prisoner I was let down by world literature. No one came to my
rescue except prenologists, authors who had been in prison—and
Tolstoy.

Quite naturally, I was eager to read any prison memoirs I
could get hold of. For example, I read the verse and prose visions
of Wilde and the fragmentary notes of Verlaine, which seemed
authentic just because they were written by exhibitionists. The
recollections of the Hungarian Kazinczy, of his seven years imprisonment, although written about a hundred and fifty years
ago, absorbed me as much as if they had been describing my
own plight. Since my release my interest in the collections of
others who have gone through political imprisonment, has
fluctuated. There have been phases of interest when I read them
because the experiences described seemed to relate directly to
myself, and others when I read for escape. I felt that I was getting the best of both worlds by reading the prison recollections
of the past: I could combine my desire to see my own fate
mirrored with that of forgetting about it. I read Silvio Pellico's
memoirs with wistful delight after some reviewers had paid me
the compliment of comparing them to mine. There was no
doubt that as a writer I was in quite good company, many of my

fellow prisoners, forerunners as well as contemporaries, had stolen my thunder—or at least a bit of it.

But it was only Tolstoy, not even a fellow prisoner at that, who I felt had made my own records seem almost superfluous. The others succeeded in depicting what was unique to prison; he knew that it was like the world outside, only more intensely so. He found in it, as every aware person had to, Guignol, and God, or His absence, occasional romance and the Law or lack of it : but he also saw, and made his readers see the misery of people broken down by punitive slavery, becoming more barren and at the same time more intense. It is not the shackled limbs of the deportees that haunts the mind of the Tolstoyan hero as he escorts them on their journey to Siberia : it is the face of the sleeping youth breathing heavily through his mouth by the dripping sanitary bucket. It is not the lack of air that induces his imprisoned *narodnik* revolutionary to commit suicide : it is a whiff from the world outside—a conversation with a new prisoner in which he suddenly realizes how he has lost touch with the world. The fug and decay, spread out in life, are concentrated in prison; it is misery that can only be overcome by taking it humbly.

Tolstoy knew everything; he knew many things wrongly. He was infallible as a narrator, as a poet of realistic epics in comfortable prose; in this field he was second to none and he knew it. He could not stand his own greatness and, to atone for it, he made himself into an unbearable apostle. He never tired of proclaiming that literature was over-rated. He tried to be good and sometimes managed it. His teachings, though they were morally impeccable and, on the whole useful, smacked of unctuousness and were often as platitudinous as they were paradoxical. Neither in his role as a Saint or thinker did he match his ability as a craftsman. Yet he was a giant spirit and his art cannot be separated from his moralizing. At the bottom of both lay his response to every bit of living flesh; countess, peasant or horse. However erroneous his judgments he was aware of what went on inside every creature he observed. No wonder he thought he was God, though he did not admit it. He professed humility and did his best to set an example. He called upon God : did he believe in him? Gorki, quite rightly, assumes that he did in a way : he felt that *he* could do without him but the rest of mankind couldn't.

Was this haughtiness or modesty, arrogance or humility? It was, of course, both. I cannot share in his haughtiness since I have not written *War and Peace*—nor am I haughty enough to pretend to be as humble as he was. In any case, I do not think that giant spirits have necessarily the best intellects. Tolstoy thought both Shakespeare and Goethe over-rated; to him they were great poets 'only'. In rather a different way this applies to Tolstoy too. Moreover his sect was irritating. The Tolstoyan beard plus sandals was as repellant then as is the Beatnik beard plus winkle-pickers today : but all uncomfortable beards are the heralds of some truth as well as of some idiosyncracy. One has no right to ridicule the weakness without recognizing the truth behind it.

The truth lying behind the Tolstoyan beard was what I would call the postulate of biological democracy. It consists of the vague but stubborn belief that all plasms on earth, and possibly on other stars or planets, are of the same order and that no person is entitled to dissassociate himself from their community. I feel co-responsible for all suffering : for that of the mouse in the cat's claws as well as for that of the cat missing his prey. Where a choice has to be made between conflicting responsibilities, I happen to be frivolous enough to opt for the cat's pleasure; where-as a Tolstoyan would opt for the more humane but less human device of trying to convert the cat to vegetarianism and the mouse to chastity. Tolstoy was not altogether a Tolstoyan : he tried to convert the Tzar and his government to a rule of greater tolerance and charity but he also quite obviously shared his heroes' pleasure in hounding a miserable wolf or sniping at French soldiers. At the bottom of his false humility which served as a shield for his pride, lay his genuine humility—a soul that was one with all souls.

The lesson is that one should be humble. I did not learn this from the stones, bricks and gratings that stood between me and life for a seeming eternity. I read it in books. But my response to that lesson might have been slower if I had not been assisted by the thugs of the Political Police.

SURRENDER, LIKE MARRIAGE

By Russell Braddon

SURRENDER, like marriage, is an estate into which one should enter only after examining its consequences most scrupulously : for, like marriage, surrender is binding and supremely personal, its consequences difficult to escape, its duration impossible to anticipate.

Therefore, as in contemplation of marriage, when contemplating surrender one should always take careful note of the habits and disposition of one's prospective captor and then ask oneself : 'Am I really ready for this new way of life? Have I really done everything possible to justify my embarking upon it?'

Here, however, the analogy ends, because whereas marriage begins, usually, with a moment of bliss, surrender begins, usually, with a moment of abject humiliation : abject humiliation as one holds up one's hands and—from that enemy whom, an instant earlier, one would have slaughtered without compunction—begs mercy.

There is no logical reason why the enemy should show mercy because, until this instant, he too has been hell-bent on slaughter : on the slaughter, in fact, of him who now holds up his hands. Thus, in the would-be prisoner-of-war, the emotion of abject humiliation is swiftly superseded, as he realizes the irrelevance of his posture, by one of acute anxiety. Will the enemy, he wonders desperately, respond to this totally illogical gesture of

44

upheld hands and be merciful? Or will he, much more sensibly and naturally, shoot the surrenderer dead?

It is precisely because of this second and most precarious stage of the process of becoming a prisoner-of-war that it is advisable, as in marriage, to have taken note of the habits and disposition of one's prospective captors.

To the soldiers of some nations it is possible to surrender with almost total confidence. The British and the Americans, for example, are thoroughly reliable, indeed *desirable*, prospective captors. As their prisoner, anybody who surrenders to them will, almost certainly in the case of the British, and quite certainly in the case of the Americans, be better fed, better clothed and much safer than he ever was as a member of the armed forces of his own country.

On the other hand, the Japanese as prospective captors are so unreliable that only in direct circumstances—and then with no optimism at all—should surrender to them be even contemplated. Moreover, should a Japanese captor be so un-Japanese, in the event of one's surrendering to him, as to spare the life of his captive, his ideas as to what constitute reasonable conditions of captivity thereafter are so un-Anglo-American as to make him an unreliable prospective enemy as well.

Between the feather-bed comforts of Anglo-American captivity and the suicidal conditions of surrender to the Japanese, there are, of course, many gradations.

The Germans are reasonably correct captors. The French, allegedly, are only slightly less so, unless one happened to be an Algerian—but those days are over now. Italians are good because they are easily bribed and not as difficult to escape from as the Germans and French. Spaniards have a rather nasty reputation as prospective captors and anyway their gaols are deplorable. Asiatics are too unpredictable, except for the Chinese who very predictably will either shoot their prisoners-of-war or brainwash them. Africans have an appalling record. Latin-Americans are excitable—but fortunately unlikely to out-fight any other race. The Russians are reluctant and inhospitable. And so it goes on.

In short, ideally one should surrender to the British or to the Americans, but if one happens *to be* either British or American —which would make such a surrender technically difficult— one's best chance is to surrender to either the Germans or the Italians. In the distressing event of Britain and America being at war with a power which is not either Germany or Italy, the prospective prisoner-of-war should at once become a conscientious objector and go down the mines of his own homeland where he will not be called upon to surrender to anyone.

But, since the theme of this chapter is not *How Not to Become a Prisoner-of-War,* we digress. Let us return to the man who has. Once this man has survived the first two stages of surrender— abject humiliation at what he is proposing and acute anxiety lest his proposal be brutally rejected—then swiftly he enters upon the third stage of his self-elected future, which is captivity. And his will be a captivity of a kind unique in many ways from any other manner of incarceration.

In the first place, his sentence, unlike any civil or even most political sentences, is indeterminate. He does not know, and cannot possibly know, whether his captivity will endure for six weeks or for six years—or even for sixty. All he knows is that only three circumstances can end it : an escape, his own death, or the end of the war. Inevitably, then, he will ignore altogether the possibility of terminating his captive state by death—for, unlike civil prisoners, prisoners-of-war practically never commit suicide, and, like all fighting men, they never expect sudden death to come to them—and will concentrate instead on one or both of the alternative circumstances, which are escape or the end of the war.

And here again a sensible, advance assessment of the nature of one's prospective captor will pay dividends, because no prospective prisoner-of-war who is also a prospective escaper should ever contemplate surrendering to a race whose colour or national physique is conspicuously different from his own. A Frenchman may well make his way out of a Greek prison compound and return, undetected, if very lucky, across a hostile central Europe to France.

So might an American escape from an Italian camp and reach England, or a Hungarian from an English camp and reach Budapest : but no European can confidently hope, in time of total war, to escape from an Asiatic camp, make his way undetected across Asia to Europe and return home. No Ghanaian can hope, mingling unobtrusively with Germans, to escape from Germany and return to Africa. No number of forged official documents will persuade a black nation that a white escapee is negroid, nor a white nation that a negro escapee is, as the Americans so charmingly express it, Caucasian.

The prospective escaper, therefore, must be careful to be captured in the right country or his war will be totally in vain. Fortunately, very few prospective escapers are incorrigible when they find that they have foolishly surrendered to a race or in a country where, by virtue of their height, colouring and physiognomy, escape is out of the question. When this is the case, about 1% of them persist in heroic but rash attempts and are soon executed; the other 99% accept the disagreeable truth of captivity in an alien land and look only to the third means whereby their captivity may be terminated—the end of the war.

In the case of Anglo-Saxon prisoners-of-war, of course, what they invariably mean by the 'end of the war' is 'victory'. This is a curious aspect of their national arrogance and stupidity which all their captors in all wars find infuriating. Confront a British prisoner-of-war with the news that the whole of England except Clapham Common—indeed the whole of the Commonwealth except Bondi Beach, one Rocky mountain and a forgotten Maori settlement—have been occupied by his enemy, and he will say : 'All right : so we'll win the war by Christmas.'

At first his captors will think that he is joking, and then that he is trying to be insolent : but finally they will accept that he means it—and will love him none the more because of that.

And when Christmas comes and still only Clapham Common, Bondi Beach, the sole Rocky and the forgotten Maoris are free, the Briton's captors will be made no happier because at once, without the slightest air of disappointment or infallibility, their captive will tell them : 'Easter, it'll be over. We'll win the war by Easter.'

This unendearing British trait is, in fact, a natural bi-product of the second circumstance by which prisoners-of-war confinement is distinguished from any civil confinement. Prisoners-of-war, however well they behave, know that there can be no remission of sentence, no pardons, no paroles. Therefore, confronted with an indeterminate imprisonment, which reason tells them could last forever, they unreasonably ordain their own remissions.

'We'll be out by Christmas,' . . . 'We'll be out by Easter,' . . . 'By August Bank holiday' . . . 'By Christmas,' they vow, successively.

Thus the indeterminate is made determinate, the limitless limited : thus the hopeless is rendered full of hope : and the instant one mad hope is dead, the next—like a king—must be proclaimed.

Until, one day, it comes true : then the Briton turns to his captor and says : 'Told you so. Told you we'd win by August,' . . . and cannot be contradicted.

This is not to say that only the British, as prisoners-of-war expect victory : rather that only the British expect it so blindly in the face of all the facts, and always at three monthly intervals. To a lesser extent, it is natural for prisoners-of-war of any race—except the Italians—at least to pretend that they expect victory; for all prisoners-of-war live, to one degree or another, with the knowledge that they have failed those of their fellow countrymen who did not surrender—those who died or those who fought on, and still fight—and such a failure will be less of a failure if its duration is brief.

This sense of failure is limited or aggravated, of course, entirely by the individual's knowledge of the causes and circumstances of his own capture. The man, who is captured whilst unconscious from wounds naturally feels less shame than the man who found himself too frightened either to fight or to flee, and instead held up his hands.

The man who fought till he had no more ammunition and then surrendered feels perhaps more justified in his surrender than the man who had ammunition left but was so hopelessly out-gunned and out-manoeuvred that to fire another shot would only have meant his own death.

Every prisoner-of-war, sooner or later—and there is always plenty of time—has to pass judgment on himself on many charges : but none will acquit himself of one of those charges at least—that he no longer fights the enemy whilst his country does. Therefore he will punish himself, and praise his fellow countrymen who still fight, by saying : *'They,'* not I—'will win.' And when the war is over it will always be, for him, a war which they, not he, won. Indeed, they will win the war he lost.

This sombre and humbling knowledge comes early in captivity—usually in its first and most traumatic weeks. Thereafter the prisoner adjusts and compensates.

'At least,' he can and does tell himself, 'though I am confined, I am not confined as civil or political prisoners are. They are confined for offences against their own people or System : I, however unavailingly, at least for a time, fought for my own people and system. They are confined by their own people : I am confined by the enemy. They are and will be ostracized : I will always be a respected member of my own community.'

Thus, suddenly, he perceives that there is available to him, in the apparently dishonourable life of one who lives only through the clemency of his country's mortal enemy, a curious kind of honour. He may achieve honour in captivity by honouring his own country; but, to achieve this, he must win from his captors either their respect, or their fear, or both. Quite soon, therefore, he and all his colleagues, not in consultation but intuitively, will adopt a code of defiance whose object is to make the enemy respectful at least, fearful at best.

At first the code will contain errors. Some forms of defiance will be too extreme and will result in executions : so they will be modified, because not all men are heroes ready to accept death for a code—and this code must be practicable for, and within the moral capabilities of, the whole community. Other forms of defiance will be abandoned as undesirable because the effort involved is disproportionate to the results achieved. But in the end there will be a code, unwritten, universally accepted and almost universally practised : and it will be a code the captor will not like.

This is the moment when a prisoner-of-war camp comes to life. Until now the captors have been totally dominant, their prisoners merely pleading to be fed, servile bodies to be counted on daily parades—the spiritless spoils of war. But now, abruptly, the prisoners become the real community and the captors become merely its armed villains. At best, now, the captors can hope for moral equality : in a well organized camp, where morale is high, moral superiority will actually lie with the prisoners. Thus used the French prisoners of Colditz to chant loudly : *'Ou sont les allemands'*, and their Polish colleagues to reply, equally loudly : 'Dans la merde'—an antiphony that infuriated their German guards.

Thus used the British prisoners of Changi to contradict the frequent Japanese assertion that Tojo was 'Number One' by saying : 'Tojo number one hundred : Churchill Number One.' Such repartee invariably earned them a bashing : but invariably it was used. Stock line : stock retort : stock result—but part of the code in a community, once numbed with shame and shock, which had now come to life. Now, once again, like his fellow countrymen who had *not* surrendered, the prisoner of war was fighting.

Catastrophically, in some instances, this does not happen :

the identification with those who fight is not made : the determination to defy is not discovered. Jewry, under Hitler's Third Reich, for example, found moral stamina only in the Warsaw Ghetto. American prisoners-of-war in North Korea seldom discovered it in time or in sufficient numbers. Both paid a frightful price—the Jews with the Kapo System that was inflicted upon them, the Americans with an unprecedented record of collaboration that haunts them to this day.

Neither learnt the essential lesson of becoming members of a captive *community* which holds its captors in contempt. The Jews, fatally, sought no wider a bond than that of family : the Americans had no common bond at all : and neither sufficiently hated the captor. Yet without this hatred all captivity will to some extent demoralize; and in the harshest conditions it will destroy utterly. Thus Americans in Korea were demoralized, Jews in Europe obliterated.

Conversely, however, under Nazi occupation, the Danes demonstrated magnificently the effectiveness of the code when, led by their king, the whole population wore yellow stars of David rather than allow a minority of Danish Jews to become instantly identifiable because only they wore the incriminating arm band. And it is one of the fortifying aspects of prisoner-of-war life that its tendencies are much more likely to be Danish than Kapo-ish or collaborationist.

There is much evidence in writing that this is so; but, for the main, its truth is not widely appreciated either because the nature of captivity itself is so esoteric as to be almost incommunicable to those who have not experienced it, or because the evidence itself sounds more apocryphal than convincing.

There is, for example, the story of the English-speaking German commandant of a camp housing mainly captured officers of the Royal Air Force. This gentleman was recognized by his flock as being as benevolent as the system allowed, but even he, when he learnt that the prisoners for whom he was responsible were nightly listening to the B.B.C. news, had to be stern.

He therefore called them on to the parade ground and, in English, advised them that he had incontrovertible evidence that they listened nightly to the B.B.C.; that this was expressly forbidden by the Führer, upon penalty of death; but that if they surrendered their secret radio set to him he would regard the matter as closed and there would be no reprisals.

The non-prisoner must be inclined to feel that, since the existence of the radio was known, and since the penalty for its discovery would be death, the commandant was being magnanimous and that his prisoners would be ill-advised to reject his offer, especially since they trusted him and knew that, if they did surrender their radio, the matter would end there.

This common sense attitude, however, ignores the prisoner-of-war code. Instead, therefore, of compliance, the commandant was greeted with loud instantaneous howls of protest. How could he, the prisoners shouted, even think that they would disobey the Führer by listening to a forbidden radio?

Patiently the commandant explained that he *knew* they listened to a forbidden radio. Patiently he again asked for its surrender. Only to be greeted once more with heckling, shouts and protests.

At which, in what he considered their own vernacular, he made his last plea.

'You have a radio,' he said. 'Give it to me. You see, gentlemen, the trouble with you is that you think I know bugger *nothing*. Actually, I know bugger *all*!'

At which his parade broke up in hopeless and hilarious disorder—and the known but secret radio never was discovered by any of the commandant's subsequent searches for it.

All of which is simply to say that confinement for prisoners-of-war reverses the virtues expected during confinement from prisoners of society. Society's prisoner is expected to be of good behaviour, to obey implicitly, to exist patiently, to conform respectfully : and the prisoner himself appreciates that this is his only hope of remission during his sentence and of social acceptance after it.

Conversely, however, the prisoner-of-war knows that if he is to obtain the respect of his captors and emerge from captivity with the respect of his fellow countrymen—not to mention his own self-respect—he must, as far as is reasonable without inflicting reprisals on his fellow sufferers, disobey constantly, exist impatiently and conform not at all.

More than this, what at home would be a crime will, in captivity, become virtuous. Thus the prisoner-of-war tells his captor lies which are as black as they are frequent. For this his chaplain will praise him as sincerely as will his senior officer. Thus the prisoner-of-war will bribe his guards and thereafter blackmail them. For this he will not be prosecuted by his community but rather provided with the means of further bribery and blackmail. Thus the prisoner-of-war, with the cunning and zeal of an incorrigible thief, will steal : and the more he steals, the more daring his thefts, the more accomplished his felonious techniques, the more his companions will admire him.

Which being the case, it is not surprising that, over a period of years, prisoners-of-war become superbly skilled and properly honoured for their art in the crimes of forgery, misrepresentation, black-marketing and larceny.

Curiously it was in the matter of thieving that Anglo-Saxon prisoners-of-war most belied their traditional traits. The English, notoriously a race who respect team work, stole always as individuals; stole silently, secretly and with an eerie capacity for becoming invisible.

Their dour compatriots, the Scots, however, stole not with dourness but with a savage bravado, relying for success not upon stealth but upon taking so openly and naturally that nobody who watched them—and usually their crimes were watched— saw any criminal intent in the observed act. But again, like the English, the Scots stole alone.

Whilst the Australians, so notoriously undisciplined and

individualistic, worked carefully in teams to achieve well planned coups.

In the best organized Japanese camps, at least, these national techniques were swiftly recognized by those who needed anything stolen. Thus, if what was required was quinine from a Japanese barrack, in which a party of prisoners was working, the best man to assign to its theft would be an Englishman. Duly, then, the Englishman concerned would suddenly vanish into thin air—and return to his camp with a bottle of quinine tablets.

But if the quinine was closely guarded day and night by a suspicious sentry whose one task was to ensure that quinine was not stolen, then the man to assign to the theft would be a Scot. Somehow, then, the Scot would contrive to lift the drug from under the sentry's nose and so deliver it to his fevered companions back in camp.

Finally, though, should the commodity required be large, firmly secured, or both, it was the Australians who were assigned to its removal. In their time, in Malaya, Australian prisoners-of-war brought back to their prisons numerous batteries from Japanese trucks (batteries used to run radios), a machine gun from a Japanese aircraft, a large, army field radio and a grand piano. Not only brought them back but, by practised misdirection, successfully slipped them through Japanese search parties of practised thoroughness.

Yet nothing better epitomises the virtue and the virtuosity of stealing as a prisoner-of-war than the case of the Scot who, from the Japanese offices in Changi Gaol, in 1944, stole a typewriter.

A column of near-naked prisoners was being marched past these offices towards the gaol's main gate. As they marched, this Scot, clad only in a kilt, swerved smartly out of the column and walked firmly into an office where a Japanese clerk sat at a desk, a typewriter in front of him.

Straight up to the desk the Scot proceeded, there smiled,

bowed, lifted the typewriter off the desk, about-turned, walked out of the office, rejoined the column, marched two miles down to the aerodrome where he was to work, the typewriter casually under his arm—and sold it to a Chinese black-marketeer for a thousand dollars, with which, by buying extra food, he was able to keep himself and his own particular group of friends alive for several months.

It is not inapposite to the subject of military confinement generally that this feat involved both theft and food—for if defiance is the mainstay of the captive's morale, food is the mainstay of his survival : and, unless one has surrendered wisely, food is quite possibly a mainstay one's captors will not be anxious to provide. In which case, the prisoner's morale must be sufficiently high both to steal dangerously and to eat unpleasantly.

In fact, many have survived captivity only because they had the strength of mind to eat what once they would never have contemplated as food. Prisoners of the Japanese from 1942 till 1945, for example, ate hibiscus leaves and juices extracted from rank lalang grass to provide themselves with vitamin B; palm oil, never before regarded as edible, and previously used only for the manufacture of soap, for added vitamins; fungus, rubber-tree nuts and copra merely for roughage and calories; and jungle snails, snakes, frogs, cats and dogs for protein. All of these were, at one time or another, an essential part of their diet.

To civilized people living a civilized life the idea of eating most of these things is repellent, whilst that of consuming cats and dogs is downright barbaric. Yet one ate them or died—and to die a prisoner-of-war was to concede victory to one's captor.

Nevertheless, few prisoners ate cats and dogs without at least first analysing the act and exonerating themselves of almost all —but never quite all—guilt.

In the first place, they agreed, it was their duty to outlive the enemy.

In the second place, they rationalized, if it was ethical to kill and eat lambs and chickens, why were cats and dogs different? That custom had made them different, no one disputed : but that logic made them the same, even the most English of starving prisoners had to accept.

And, finally, that meat was the most vital element lacking in a diet which Japanese had ensured lacked almost all vital elements, was indisputable. Dogs and cats being the only real meat-bearing animals around, it was eventually agreed that they must be eaten.

The local dogs and cats were not, at first, aware of this agreement and, for a while, succumbed amiably to the wicked enticements of those who planned to consume them. Societies whom these pages are likely to outrage will, however, be glad to learn two facts.

First, no prisoner, having laid hands on one of the trusting pets of the Japanese garrison, could ever bring himself to despatch it without first stroking its head till it went to sleep. Thereupon it was handed over to a second member of the group— usually self-styled, with defensive cynicism, a 'Dog Lovers Society'—who killed it instantly, skinned it expertly and dropped it into the waiting pot.

Thereafter proceedings were fairly routine. The sweet and unaccustomed aroma of meat stew would seep through gaol corridors : the Japanese owner of the pet now stewing, made anxious by its absence, would suspect, most accurately, that the hated Britishers were about to eat it : he would storm into the gaol and, too late, detect the scent of cooking : the prisoners would be warned of his arrival and, cooking pot in hand, would flee all round the gaol ahead of him until their fragrant trail was hopelessly confused : the animal would finally be consumed : and, for the next few weeks, those who had consumed it would suffer less from skin diseases, debility, fever and starvation.

The second fact which will hearten Societies dedicated to the protection of animals is that dogs and cats, if at first unsuspecting, did not remain unsuspecting for long : and, having lost their innocence, became extremely difficult to inspire with even the smallest flicker of trust. And yet, most curiously, the moment the war ended, these same animals, as if telepathically aware that now they were safe from such monstrous abnormalities as the cooking pot, flocked back to the now friendly company of those who, only the day before, would have eaten them.

Thus sustained, many thousands of men survived periods of captivity which all existing medical knowledge clearly stated to be impossible to survive. It was not, however, their exotic diet alone which kept them alive : complementing this diet there had to be a pigheaded and totally unreasonable will not to die.

This—it must be noticed—is quite different from the will to live, which too often ignores the presence of death. The will not to die recognizes that death is at hand, acknowledges frankly that death is right to expect another victim, and then refuses to become such a victim. Survivors of Buchenwald and Dachau acquired this will exactly as survivors of the Thailand Railway acquired it. Nazis were no less perplexed by it than were the Japanese : and no one can properly understand it who has not experienced it.

Many laymen attempt, glibly, to explain it as a reward for a profound faith in one's God. One prayed for mercy, they explain, and God granted mercy. It is a nice thought, an idealistic thought : but it is not the truth. The truth is that most men who survived the worst concentration camps of World War II did so either as agnostics or as atheists—and all of them survived by calling only upon a spark *within* themselves; for to kneel and beseech extra strength from any power *outside* of oneself was to concede victory to death at once.

The clearest explanation of the nature of this will not to die, which is inexplicable, is a negative one. In concentration camps all over the world many men lived for year after year, defying all the laws of normal mortality, rejecting the temptation of an extinction which, compared with the conditions they endured, and were apparently to endure forever, was merciful. Abruptly,

though, each of these thousands made his individual decision—
to abandon the will not to die.

The decision made, the events that followed were always the
same. That night the prisoner would lie down as he had hundreds of nights before, emaciated, hideous, barely alive. And the
next morning he would be dead. He would be survived by companions no less emaciated, maltreated or diseased than himself :
but whereas he had determined not to live any longer, they had
not yet determined to die.

One of the stranger aspects of this decision—horrifying to
those who witnessed it, for it was easily recognizable—was the
way those who had taken it so often refused to accept the last
meal to which they were entitled. It was almost as if, having
eaten everything and anything to survive thus far, they now, as
they turned their backs on survival, offered their last portion of
food to those others who still wished to outwit death.

In vain, in those days, did one collect the night's meagre
ration of food for a companion who suddenly, unexpectedly,
obviously and irrevocably had lain down to die. In vain did one
plead and bully to make him eat.

'You eat it,' he would say, indifferently.

Then, refusing to talk, or to listen, disinterested in prayer or
comfort—yet often, symbolically, folding his hands over his
chest—he would close his eyes. And die.

Frequently, too, when one thus died, his friend soon followed
him. Lacking all other possessions, and any other comfort or en-
couragement, the survivor felt unendurably lonely in a camp that
housed thousands, and himself sought extinction. Aware of this,
if only in a subconscious or animal way, men fought to keep
their friends alive even more bitterly than they did to survive
themselves.

On the whole, however, prisoners-of-war are spared the
hideous disfiguration of body and mind which are inflicted in
Nazi concentration camps and on Thailand's Railway. Much
more generally they exist in conditions which, though harsh,

are endurable, the worst features of which are, as has been said, that one lives only because of one's captor's clemency, and that one has no idea how long this disagreeable state will endure.

Yet still there will be a scar; and, worse, it will be self-inflicted. Having established a *modus vivendi* with his captors, the prisoner invariably sets about committing infallibly to memory the *modus vivendi* he knew outside captivity. He will torture his mind, and interrogate all his friends, until he has remembered the position and name of every main building in the city that to him was home. He will narrate to his friends, and repeat endlessly, every detail of his past life, and then listen to their similar, endless repetitions. He will reconstruct for them the plot of every book he has read, every play or film he has seen, and then listen to their similar reconstructions. And by doing so he will rigidly condition himself over the ensuing years to the modes and mentality of the day when he was captured.

In his desperate attempts not to lose the memory of the freedom he once had, the prisoner-of-war who was captured in 1940, by 1945 had often sealed himself inescapably in a mental capsule of the thirties. For him, in 1945, the world was and would become again the world of the thirties: yet, lamentably for his peace of mind, to the rest of the world the thirties had been as transient as the twenties and all that mattered now was the latest life of 1945.

His mind inflexibly attuned to past times, the prisoner-of-war will thus always and inevitably, and increasingly with each year of captivity, re-enter society at a loss to understand it. For him there will be a total and exaggerated loss of that continuity of modern life which alone, because of its pace, makes 'today' comprehensible to the man experiencing it.

Fortunately, however, he has also had to acquire in captivity the habit of adaptability—because life in any prisoner-of-war camp is made domestically tolerable only by the most ingenious of improvisations—and so, after ten years or so, he may appear to be completely re-integrated. Nevertheless, there will always be a hiatus—and to a lesser or greater degree he will always resent it.

He will resent it that the slang to which he returns is not the slang he left behind; and though he adapts quickly to it, as he did to his captor's foreign tongue, he will be a long time accepting it. The universal use of the phrase 'couldn't care less', in 1945, drove returning prisoners-of-war almost insane because it reflected an approach to life which, to him in the past few years, would have meant death.

He will resent it that customs have changed at home, even though he adapted, and expected endlessly to have to adapt, to different customs in captivity. Whereas most British servicemen wanted no more of Churchill as Prime Minister in the election of 1945, almost all British prisoners-of-war were appalled that he was dismissed from office, purely because the change to Attlee meant a change *from* the world they had left behind. Indeed, for days, they refused to believe that he had been dismissed and regarded the story—even though it came from the B.B.C.—as some weird form of Japanese propaganda.

Australian prisoners-of-war, who had for almost four years made do with a starvation diet and a complete lack of amenities, bitterly resented returning home to rationed food and the employment of women in the Forces. They resented these things not out of continuing hunger or conspicuous chivalry, but simply because these were not the things they had left behind.

In other ways, though, the ex-prisoner-of-war will usually have benefited from his captivity. Usually, in his desire to obliterate the sense of personal failure which the act of surrender had induced in him, the prisoner-of-war attempts to increase his knowledge, sharpen or discover a particular talent, broaden his education.

Foreign languages (rarely, though, that of the captor power) are studied and mastered. Lectures by experts are given in courses on everything from contract law to communism, from the Bible to economics—and are largely and regularly attended.

Indeed Changi Gaol, in 1944, offered the refreshing spectacle of an audience most of which, with great impartiality, attended courses on both communism and the Bible, whilst believing in neither.

The habit of reading books, and valuing books, becomes almost universal.

An enthusiasm for live theatre is quickly born in men denied all cinemas, radios and television sets.

A capacity at least to listen to great music is acquired even by those who once liked only popular music, because, as the years pass, the pops of yesterday grow very stale—and there is no way of hearing the latest recordings of today.

In a community of thousands there is always someone who is an expert on any required subject : and as the stomach shrinks through inadequate feeding, the mind, strangely, in those determined to survive, always becomes more anxious to reach the mind of that other man who knows something new.

Thus, and particularly in camps under the unbenevolent rule of the Japanese, a sort of cultural fever, as rapid as malaria itself, often beset whole captive communities.

Changi's taste in theatre, for example, was very demanding. By 1944 its inmates had progressed so far beyond the normal camp farce that they wanted all the plays that had been hits on the pre-war West End stage of London. But before these could be provided, there were two slight difficulties to overcome. First, there was no theatre in which they could be played : secondly, there were no copies available of the text of any of these plays.

At once plans were submitted to the Japanese for the building of a stage and an open air auditorium in one of the gaol courtyards.

'Draw the plans,' one of the originators of the concept urged, 'on a very small piece of paper, then they'll think it's a very small stage.'

This was done and the Japanese, looking at the very small

piece of paper, and well aware that there were no building materials available anyway, gave their consent.

In the ensuing months thousands of square feet of timber and canvas and corrugated iron, hundreds of electric light bulbs, miles of steel wire and sufficient bolts and nuts were stolen from the Japanese themselves to build a wide stage above which, to a height of forty feet, all scenery could be 'flown', an orchestra pit, storage space, ample dressing accommodation and open air seats for a large audience.

Confronted with all of this, the Japanese commandant remarked: 'I gave permission for you to build a small stage—not a sky-scraper,' and then waited for the first show.

But how to perform '*Autumn Crocus*' with no script? The answer was simple, if laborious. From the entire gaol community, all those who had ever acted in *Autumn Crocus,* or seen *Autumn Crocus,* or read it, contributed what they remembered of it. Gradually the script grew—and prompted further recollections, or alterations—until at last it was whole. And others followed. And all were produced.

Yet, in spite of this frenzy of intellectual stimulation, which is one of the bi-products of captivity, the captive mind is seldom creative. Great novels, or plays, or poems, or music seem not to be written in prisoner-of-war camps—or even in concentration camps: rather, past novels, plays, poems and music are re-studied and reproduced. The captive mind is academic at best: at worst, it is too frightened of forgetting its immediate past to have any creative thought about either the stark present or the elusive future. New schools of acting do not arise to match the superb ingenuity with which stages and scripts are provided to sustain the actors. Fresh facets of old problems or virtues are not apparent to those obsessed only with the old *status quo*. Life is too harshly practical to permit speculation. A *Mein Kampf* will never emerge from a Ravensbruck. Military confinement kills research and induces only a desire to reassert what is already known.

Except perhaps in the art of living together—which it often raises to a level unknown in normal society or in society's more normal penal institutions.

It is at this level that the unwritten prisoner's code becomes most sophisticated. Virtually it declares that there is only one kind of crime—the act that hurts the rest of the community. Of almost all other human failings or idiosyncrasies it is so tolerant that it does not even waste time gossiping about them. But to him who wantonly or stupidly brings fruitless reprisals or difficulties upon the camp as a whole, it is inflexibly harsh.

This, again, is something so subtle that it can only be explained by examples from camps that were exceptional in their frightfulness. In these camps all men helped all men, not so much because they loved one another as because each man who fell into helplessness decreased the general morale of the camp, increased the number of flies bearing disease from his fouled bed space, and inflamed the captor's instinct for brutality.

In Thailand men boiled every drop of water before they drank it : but they did this not so much because they wanted to protect *themselves* from cholera as because of the fact that, if they did catch cholera, they would doubtless, by their defecations and vomiting, infect and kill half a dozen others. To kill oneself was always permissible : to kill others was barbarous.

So the man who did not help his fellow man, or who did not boil his water, was punished with the one punishment that is effective in conditions already hyper-penal; hatred. And it is a rare villain who, when he weighs ninety pounds or less, when he is battered, diseased and far from home, finds the benefits of villainy worth hatred.

But the two wickedest crimes in the concentration camp calendar are nothing to do with death or the body; they are solely to do with the mind. They are the crimes of undeserved privilege or non-fulfilled responsibility.

The useless prisoner-of-war will be cheerfully tolerated and sustained by all his companions : but the man who by any means

—from asserting his rank to collaborating with the enemy; from not doing a job he could do to funking a job he should do—will be detested. The Jewish Kapo who flogged his fellow Jews to secure for himself better food and accommodation in Nazidom's concentration camps was no worse, nor any more hated, than the senior officer who insisted on privilege without responsibility in any prisoner-of-war camp. The traitor in wartime was no more despicable than the prisoner who kept drugs he did not yet need for himself when someone else, lacking them, died. The enemy himself was not so contemptible as he who, given the job of carrying food or water into a camp, and given it under a guarantee of safety from the enemy, then sold that water to his dying companions instead of sharing it among them.

That some men did all of these things in the camps of World War II is indisputable. What is also indisputable is that all of them are known, all of them were hated, all of them are still hated and none of them have prospered.

And just as the only effective deterrent from crime against the community was hate, so the only reward for extreme service and courage was affection—and that bestowed as rarely as earldoms or Victoria Crosses in more conventional communities. Every camp had its hero and its saint; and all the inmates of those camps offered that hero or saint only one thing—affection. Ironically those thus rewarded were very seldom those subsequently honoured by officialdom or in Military Gazettes: but no official decoration can strengthen the honour of a camp's affection, nor can it deflect the venom of a camp's hatred.

Between those loved and those hated, of course, lie the vast majority who simply conformed to the code. Though some achieved miracles—making paper out of grass, toothbrushes out of coconut bristle, nails out of the spikes on barbed wire, radios out of scrap, surgical instruments out of bamboo, escape documents out of impossible material, escape tunnels in spite of every supervision — sabotaging — defying — entertaining — though they did all of this, they did merely what was expected of them.

They were part of the ant community, living a most complex communal life, and their only reward was that, when they returned to freedom, they did so with some self-respect.

'*Returned to freedom*', one writes, and realizes that here, for all who were or will become prisoners-of-war, is the nub of the matter; for the essence of that life is not what its conditions and spirit were or may be, but what those conditions and the spirit will make of life outside, at home.

To the returning prisoner-of-war there must always be many advantages stemming from captivity as he starts civilian life again. For one thing, he has criteria of black experiences compared with which the average hardship of normal life will seem trivial.

For another, having experienced the nadir of personal freedom and his right to express himself, he will always be possessed of a tremendous incentive either to succeed in life or to enjoy life as it is.

He will return with a prison camp education behind him more valuable probably, and based on a curriculum infinitely wider certainly, than any University could give him.

He will know himself as deeply and as pitilessly as could any psychiatrist or analyst.

But he will still find, to his consternation, that the great and immutable laws of the code that protected and kept him alive in captivity no longer prevail in freedom.

Angrily then he will demand, of himself at least, if not of the world, why, if these ideals could exist in the squalor and privation of the camp from which he has just emerged, can they not continue in the much kinder climate of free society?

Free society will not answer him because it will not know what he is talking about—although blitzed London could remember if it wished—and he will not be able to solve the problem for himself because both the principles of his captivity and the blessed pre-war world he committed to memory as a captive are sacrosanct and not even to be criticized, still less modified.

Also, he will find that he is very old, and proportionately older according to the harshness of the captive conditions he survived; this not in terms of academic knowledge but of physical experience. He will know death as doctors and nurses and the mortally ill know it. He will know charity as the bed-ridden and indigent know it. He will know drunken elation as the chronic alcoholic knows it—and despair as the dope addict knows it. He will have practised the ruthless cunning of the thief just as regularly as he has the last rites of the priest. He will have passed judgment on a thousand men—and on himself. He will have known the nightmare of starvation and the exquisite anticipation of a huge meal, be it only cooked cat or fricasseed cobra. He will have witnessed the extremes of corruption and nobility, of selfishness and selflessness. And he will return to a life where none of these extremes exist except under society's solid veneer of normalcy.

Educated by his war-time past, he will need peace-time associates who combine all the qualities of doctor, priest, alcoholic, drug addict, thief, saint and villain before his mind and theirs can be *en rapport*. He will not find them : and he cannot then turn for company to the colleagues of his prison camp days because they will be scattered all over the world and, anyway, that would be to ignore the community in which he now lives. This he cannot do because the basic principle of his code is that one must live in, with and for the community.

An old man, he will be : and yet, as far as 'home' is concerned, because his experience of it stopped the day he left it, and was then committed to memory, he will be less than his true age. He will still be the much younger man who first went into captivity. An old, young, immature man who—as far as the lost years are concerned—might just as well have been in a state of suspended animation, frozen in an old-fashioned block of ice.

And soon, perhaps, he will develop into a bitter old-young-immature man, because he has experienced something dynamic and traumatic, and there is no one with whom he can share it. So, in the end, his friends will say : 'No, he never talks about it. Don't know why, but he just shuts up like a clam.'

Or : 'Don't start him off, for God's sake. Once he starts, you'd think nothing else had ever happened.'

Sad, in both cases. Sad that the one despairs of ever conveying why he had to sit all night holding the hand of a man he did not like because one couldn't, in those days, leave him to die alone —and, despairing, won't talk at all.

Sad that the other, determined to explain the code, tells the same story of the Scot and the typewriter over and over again. The whole family and all his friends know it off by heart, and dread its repetition. And see no code in it anyway. So soon he'll tell it again, because there's a lesson there, if only they'd learn it. If only he could explain it. Why can't they see it?

It is after about three years of glorious 'peace' that there comes the period of danger. The silent ones have been silent too long; the talkative ones have talked too much—and still unavailingly.

Then the psychiatric wards in military hospitals begin to fill with ex-prisoners-of-war. The psychiatrists who question the patients seem very *young* and inexperienced to this latest batch of patients. They don't even know what a camp was like—how well it ran—how good the life was. Not the living of it, but the principles behind it. And they can't for a second understand why one should be obsessed with hatred for that *bastard* of a brigadier who did nothing to justify his rank or his idleness for years on end and then sold money to men who were dying for I.O.U.'s at the rate of one worthless dollar to a pound.

'Did you buy a dollar for a pound?' the psychiatrist will ask.

'Course not.'

'Then why are you worried . . . ?'

'My mate did. A hundred dollars for a hundred pounds.'

'Did your mate pay the hundred pounds?'

'Course he didn't.'

'Then why ... ?'

'Skip it. If you don't understand, I can't explain.'

How to explain that one can't hate *enough* a brigadier who wore his red tabs of rank and did nothing but sell worthless dollars for what he hoped, foolishly, would be valuable I.O.U's? That one can't hate enough the private who sold malaria patients water? The sergeant who did not stand between his men and the enemy's guards—though he was quick enough to insist that his men stood to attention for him? How to explain that one can't hate enough the brother officer who wouldn't wash and therefore crawled with lice that spread disease?

So the psychiatrist, acknowledging that here is a sphere of human experience unexplored by Freud or anyone else—and frankly unexplorable now, because it has vanished with the war —closes his dossier, marking it with the trite words, *'Anxiety neurosis'*.

Fortunately the ex-prisoner-of-war will soon emerge from such a fresh form of confinement because he has had too much experience of coping with captors not to be able to cope with this. He will adapt, and, having adapted, will be discharged. He will be accepted by society as having 'adjusted'.

As will those who successfully conceal what they feel and so survive the danger period. In fact, spurred on by the incentive of the nadir they have left behind, they *will* have adjusted, because they will have moulded this new life to their own way of life : more they will have succeeded in a way that both they and society can accept as successful.

But for the rest, for most, in fact, there will be neither an official anxiety neurosis nor an adjusted and accepted success. There will simply be an adaptation to a new way of life—and always, about it, the question : 'But what happened to the old way?'

The question is inevitable from the moment one holds up one's hands and begs the enemy for mercy. It becomes doubly inevitable in those seconds when one waits to be shot—

and grows old. It crystallizes in the fluid of captivity's peculiar code.

Like marriage, surrender is a very personal, final and catalytic act.

A PERSONAL AFFAIR

By Arthur Koestler

TO die—even in the service of an impersonal cause—is always a personal affair. Thus it was inevitable that these pages, written for the most part in the actual expectancy and fear of death, should bear an intimate character. There are, in the author's opinion, two reasons which justify their publication.

In the first place, the things which go on inside a condemned man's head have a certain psychological interest. Professional writers have rarely had an opportunity of studying these processes in the first person singular. I have tried to present them as frankly and concisely as I can. The main difficulty was the temptation to cut a good figure; I hope that I have succeeded in overcoming this.

In the second place, I believe that wars, in particular civil wars, consist of only ten per cent action and of ninety per cent passive suffering. Thus this account of the hermetically sealed Andalusian mortuaries may perhaps bring closer to the reader the nature of the Spanish Civil War than descriptions of battles.

I dedicate it to my friend Nicolás, an obscure little soldier of the Republic, who on April 14th, 1937, on the sixth birthday of that Republic, was shot dead in the prison of Seville.

*   *   *

In August, 1936, the first month of the Civil War, I had visited Portugal and rebel Spain for the *News Chronicle*. In Seville, at that time the insurgents' G.H.Q., I had an interview with General Queipo de Llano and ample opportunity to observe the amount of German and Italian military support for the insurgents. The evidence I collected was published by the *News Chronicle*, and later in a book entitled *L'Espagne Ensanglantée*. Never again was a representative of a British liberal paper allowed to enter rebel territory.

During my stay in Seville, Captain Bolín, in charge of the insurgents' Press Department, had acted as my cicerone. It was Bolín who had arranged my interview with General de Llano.

On the day after that interview I met a German journalist whom I had known years before in Berlin, and who was now working for Nazi papers. He knew all about my 'red' past, which was unknown to Captain Bolín. I managed to escape to Gibraltar just in time; the warrant for my arrest was issued an hour after I had crossed the frontier. Back in London, I published my material. Colleagues coming from Spain told me some months later that Captain Bolín had sworn 'to shoot K. like a mad dog if ever he got hold of him.'

It was this same Captain Bolín who arrested Chalmers-Mitchell and myself the day after the insurgents occupied Malaga.

Yet this is only one-half of the prelude to our story. The other half runs thus :

Captain Bolín had a cousin. This cousin had a house in Malaga. It was the villa next to ours.

The cousin's name was Señor Thomas Bolín. This Thomas Bolín and his entire family owed their lives to Sir Peter. Sir Peter told me how this had happened during the last dinner we had together in his house, on the night before we were arrested.

Thomas Bolín was a member of the *Requete,* the Spanish

Monarchist Party. On July 18th, 1936, the Generals launched
their insurrection throughout Spain. In Malaga as in Madrid
and Barcelona, the rebels after fierce street fighting, were defeated; the Republicans remained in control of the city, and
Señor Bolín came to the house of his neighbour, Sir Peter, whom
he knew to be a 'red', to ask for shelter and protection.

He arrived with his wife, mother-in-law, five or six children
and two or three maids. Sir Peter installed the whole Bolín tribe
in his house. Señor Bolín occupied the same two rooms which I
was to live in six months later. The Bolíns' own house was closed
down and repeatedly searched. During one of the searches,
Anarchist militiamen found some compromising documents.
Next, they found in the same drawer a set of pornographic
photographs. The leader of the search party, a young chap,
was highly pleased with both discoveries. Then Sir Peter, who
was present as a witness at the search, had a happy inspira-
tion :

'Look here,' he said to the leader, 'why not strike a bargain?
You keep the pretty pictures, and I keep these documents.'

The Anarchist was at first indignant, then amused, and finally, out of friendliness towards Sir Peter, he consented.

Some days later, nevertheless, Señor Bolín was arrested. But
Sir Peter secured his release, obtained passports for his family,
and finally, at the peril of his own life, smuggled Bolín out of
Malaga to Gibraltar.

Bolín's luggage remained in Sir Peter's house; Bolín's villa
was converted into a military hospital.

We were arrested on Tuesday, February 9th, at 11 a.m.

At 10.30 I was standing on the roof, our usual observation
post, counting the lorries full of Italian troops which were still
driving down from the mountains in an endless column. The
Italians looked fresh and well-fed. Their faultless equipment,
from steel helmet to puttees, provided a striking contrast to the
ragged, wretched garb of the Republican Militiamen.

Then I saw an elegant private car, covered with dust and

decorated with the Bourbon flag, driving up the road to Señor Bolín's house. I told Sir Peter of this.

'It must be Bolín returning from exile,' he said. 'Now it is his turn to protect *us*.'

He set out at once for the villa.

Ten minutes later he was back, looking very upset.

'It *was* Thomas Bolín,' he said. 'He's just come back by car from Gibraltar.'

'Has he got any more dirty postcards?'

'No, but he's wearing the red beret of the *Requetes,* and has a huge army revolver. He says it will give him great pleasure to hunt down the Reds in the town and kill a few of them with his own hands.'

'Did he at least say "thank you" to you?'

Sir Peter shrugged his shoulders and walked upstairs to get Señor Bolín's belongings together for him.

I was left alone in the garden. Once more I felt in urgent need of a drink of brandy, and I went into the library to get one.

The library had three doors. While I was looking for the brandy, the three doors opened simultaneously, almost noiselessly, and three officers, revolvers in their hands, entered.

Two of them were unknown to me. All I noticed was that they were wearing brand-new uniforms. The third was Captain Bolín.

What follows happened very quickly, as in a speeded-up film. The syringe was in my pocket; all I required was to be left alone for two or three minutes. Acting quite automatically, I tried to slip upstairs. When I got to the third stair a sharp voice called me back.

'Hands up!'

I raised both hands above my head, without turning round, and waited for Bolín to shoot. At the back of my skull I felt a faint, expectant itching, a sort of sucking void, not entirely unpleasant. It increased from second to second; I heard all four of us breathing loudly.

'Come down.'

I stepped down backwards with great care. 'If you stumble,' I told myself, 'you are a dead man.'

We stood in a group in the middle of the library with three revolvers pointing at me—one from each side, a third from the rear.

It was all quite dreamlike, the air hummed round me as in the hollow of a sea-shell. Through the humming I heard Captain Bolín's voice, calling to the gardener:

'A rope.'

The gardener went off to fetch one. I noticed that he was limping.

Sir Peter appeared at the top of the staircase with Señor Bolín's valise in his hand.

'Hands up.'

He put his hands up. The valise came bumping and skipping down the staircase. Then it came to a rest, and there was silence. We all stood in a frozen group, like wax-work figures at Madame Tussaud's.

Then a fourth individual, with a red cap, entered the room. I recognized him at once by his resemblance to his cousin; it was Señor Thomas Bolín. He stood looking on at the pleasant little scene with a grin on his face.

'Sir Peter,' I asked, 'is this the man whose life you saved?' Señor Bolín grinned.

The gardener came back. He had been unable to find a rope but had brought two yards of electric wiring.

'I believe they're going to hang me,' I said to Sir Peter.

It occurred to me that the final agony would be certain to last longer with this inflexible wire than it would with an ordinary rope.

'Shut up!' said Bolín. He made a sign to the officer on my left.

The officer, a handsome young man who looked rather shy and seemed to be quite a nice fellow—took the wire and planted himself behind me. He twisted my hands behind my back and tried to bind them with the wire. But the wire was too stiff. He walked round me, pulled my hands round to the front as though manipulating a wooden doll, and once more tried to tie them. Meanwhile Bolín was pressing his revolver into my right side, the third officer his into my left. This latter was a fat, bald-headed fellow with incredibly bestial features. During the whole proceeding he had a grin on his face and literally snorted with pleasure. He snorted through his nose as though he had asthma; I could feel his breath on my ear. Up till then I had only come across such sadistic types in political cartoons, and had never believed that they actually existed. He grinned and snorted and snorted. He was obviously a pathological case. My physical disgust broke the dreamlike spell, I was fully conscious again and fear returned; it crept under the skin and gripped the entrails.

Then, to my own astonishment, I heard myself saying:

'Look here, Bolín, if you're going to shoot me, take me upstairs, don't do it in Sir Peter's presence.'

Later on I often wondered whether this sentence, which may have saved my life, was prompted by consideration for Sir Peter or merely by the desire to gain time. Perhaps it was a mixture of both.

'Shut up!' said Bolín; but there was a trace of uncertainty in his voice. He must have realized that it wouldn't do, after all, to shoot a foreign journalist in a prominent Englishman's house.

The next thing I remember is Sir Peter reasoning with Thomas Bolín. He was asking if he could have five minutes conversation with him in the next room. Señor Bolín smiled sardonically, but he couldn't refuse. The two of them went into the next room. Captain Bolín supervised the complicated procedure of the binding of my hands, and then joined them. The door was left ajar. The three had a short palaver. It was obvious from their gestures that Sir Peter was pleading for me, and that he was not having much success.

7

I was not allowed to go near them.

'What's happening?' I shouted through the open door.

They came out, and Sir Peter said very quietly :

'It seems that it is all right for me, but not for you.'

Then we were taken away.

To this day I do not know what made Captain Bolín break his promise 'to shoot K. like a dog,' but evidently it all hinged on his cousin's 'pretty pictures'. At any rate I wish to acknowledge in public my gratitude to the anonymous lady who posed for them.

Malaga Prison

'*Lleva calcetines de mujer*' (wears women's stockings), the official wrote in my record. As he was doing so, I managed to catch a glimpse of the record that had been made out by Captain Bolín and was lying on the table in front of the official. I read that I was a very dangerous character—I presumed that was because of the hypodermic needle—that I should be carefully guarded and kept *incomunicado*—that is to say, isolated; and that I was a *caso internacional*—an international case, which I assumed to mean a spy. And now, to complete the record, came the 'women's stockings'.

Finally my fingerprints were taken, and I was allowed to put all my clothes on again with the exception of my belt, which was kept in the office.

Then I was taken to a cell.

For the first time I heard the sound of a cell door being slammed from the outside.

*   *   *

It was a unique sound. A cell door has no handle, either outside or inside; it cannot be shut except by being slammed to. It is made of massive steel and concrete, about four inches thick, and every time it falls to there is a resounding crash as though a shot had been fired. But this report dies away without an echo. Prison sounds are echoless and bleak.

When the door has been slammed behind him for the first time, the prisoner stands in the middle of the cell and looks round. I fancy that everyone must behave in more or less the same way.

First of all he gives a fleeting look round the walls and takes a mental inventory of the objects in what is now to be his domain :

> the iron bedstead,
> the wash-basin,
> the W.C.[1]
> the barred window.

His next action is invariably to try to pull himself up by the iron bars of the window and look out. He fails, and his suit is covered with white from the plaster on the wall against which he has pressed himself. He desists, but resolves to practise and master the art of pulling himself up by his hands. He makes some more laudable resolutions : he will do exercises every morning; and learn a foreign language; and he simply won't let his spirit be broken. He dusts his suit and continues his voyage of exploration round his realm—five paces long by four paces broad. He tries the iron bedstead. The springs are broken, the wire mattress sags and cuts into the flesh; it's like lying in a hammock made of steel wire. He pulls a humorous face, being determined to prove to himself that he is full of courage and confidence. Then his gaze rests on the cell door, and he sees that an eye is glued to the spy-hole and is watching him.

The eye goggles at him glassily, its pupil unbelievably large; it is an eye without a man attached to it, and for a few moments the prisoner's heart stops beating.

[1] A. K. is talking, of course, of a prison in backward Spain. English prisons have remained faithful to the slop system. The slops are emptied in the morning on 'slop parade'. (Ed.)

The eye disappears and the prisoner takes a deep breath and presses his hand against the left side of his chest.

'Now, then,' he says to himself encouragingly, 'how silly to go and get so frightened. You must get used to that; after all, the official's only doing his duty by peeping in; that's part of being in prison. But they won't get me down, they'll never get me down; I'll stuff paper in the spy-hole at night. . . .'

As a matter of fact there's no reason why he shouldn't do so straight away. The idea fills him with genuine enthusiasm. For the first time he experiences that almost manic desire for activity that from now on will alternate continually—up and down in a never-ending zig-zag—with apathy and depression.

Then he realizes that he has no paper on him, and his next impulse is—according to his social status—either to ring or to run over to the stationer's at the corner. This impulse lasts only the fraction of a second; the next moment he becomes conscious for the first time of the true significance of his situation. For the first time he grasps the full reality of being behind a door which is locked from outside, grasps it in all its searing, devastating poignancy.

This, too, lasts only a few seconds. The next moment the anaesthetizing mechanism gets going again, and brings about that merciful state of semi-narcosis induced by pacing and down, forging plans, weaving illusions.

'Let's see,' says the novice, 'Where are we? Ah, yes, that business of stuffing paper into the spy-hole. It must be possible to get hold of paper somehow.' He leaves the 'how' in this 'somehow' suspended in mid-air. This is a mode of thought that he will soon master—or, rather, it will master him. 'When I get out,' he will say, for example, 'I shall never worry about money again. I shall rub along somehow or other.' Or: 'When I get out, I shall never quarrel with the wife again. We'll manage to get along somehow.'

Indeed, 'somehow' everything will be all right once he's free. This stereotyped line of thought means that the outside world increasingly loses its reality for him; it becomes a vague dream world, a lost paradise in which everything is somehow possible.

'Where were we? . . . Oh, yes, that business of stuffing paper into the spy-hole.' Of course, somehow one can get hold of paper. But is it allowed? No, it's certain not to be allowed. So why bother? . . .

'Let's take a more thorough inventory of the objects in the room. Why, look, there's an iron table with a chair which we haven't observed or fully appreciated yet. Of course the chair can't be moved from the table; it's welded to it. A pity, otherwise one might use it as a bed table and put one's things on it when getting undressed—pocket-book, handkerchief, cigarettes, matches and so on. . . .'

Then it occurs to him that he has neither pocket-book nor handkerchief, cigarettes or matches in his pocket.

The barometer of his mood falls a second time.

It rises again the moment he has tried the tap over the wash-basin. 'Look, there's running water in prison—it isn't half as bad as one imagined from outside. After all there is a bed (and it's much healthier to sleep on a hard bed), a wash-basin, a table, a chair—what more does a man need? One must learn to live simply and unassumingly : a few exercises, reading, writing, learning a foreign language. . . .'

The next voyage of discovery is in the direction of the water closet. 'Why, there's even one of these—it's really not half so bad.' He pulls the plug. The chain refuses to function. And the barometer falls afresh.

It rises again once the subtle plan has been conceived of filling the bucket with water from the tap and of flushing the lavatory pan in this way. It falls again when it transpires that the tap has also ceased to function. It rises again when he reflects that there must be certain times of the day when the water runs. It falls—

it rises—it falls—it rises. And this is how things are to go on—in the coming minutes, hours, days, weeks, years.

How long has he already been in the cell?

He looks at his watch; exactly three minutes.

I believe that the majority of prisoners behave in a similar way during the first few months in the cell. The more drastic a situation, the more stereotyped the way in which people react to it. Whenever life is at its most dramatic, it is least able to escape the commonplace. At the so-called great moments of life, we have to fall back on clichés. The virtue of the word lies in the sphere of abstractions; before the concrete and tangible language pales. It becomes a completely useless instrument when it is a question of describing such horribly naked facts as the fear of a human being in the face of death.

I had hardly been five minutes in the cell when there was a rattling in the lock and the door was thrown open.

Outside, stood the two officials I had already met, the one who had searched me and the one who had entered the bit about the 'women's stockings' in my record.

'*Venga*,' they said. 'Come.'

I did not dare to ask where.

Once more we marched down the long, bare corridors, past an endless row of closed cell doors.

To every spy-hole on each side of the corridor a goggling eye was glued.

We passed through a double file of eyes—of wide-open, staring eyes, eyes without people attached to them.

The warder who had searched me was in radiant mood. He stretched out his hand in the direction of this and that cell, giving a downward sweep with his index finger.

'Bang, bang,' he said. 'Reds, Reds, the whole lot of 'em. All dead tomorrow.'

The eyes stared. Behind each hole was a pupil.

'You dead tomorrow, too,' said the warder.

I had a feeling that my knees were filled with flabby jelly. 'The condemned man walked with an uncertain gait.' All condemned men walk with an uncertain gait. I couldn't escape the blasted clichés.

At the end of the corridor was an iron grille. The official turned a lock and threw the grille back. Behind it was a shorter corridor with fewer cells : the isolation cells.

One of the cell doors was unlocked : I was given a thump in the back and hurled in. And once more the door slammed to behind me.

The fixtures were exactly the same, only the barred window was smaller and placed somewhat higher up. The wall above the iron bedstead was spattered with blood. It must have been fresh blood, for it still smelt slightly sour. I smelt it and then I was sick.

I felt utterly wretched. I lay down on the wire mattress. There was no straw palliasse and no blanket. It was bitterly cold. I was freezing, the iron network cut into all my limbs, and I could not escape that sour smell. The W.C. was blocked and the tap did not function. Through the window, I could hear isolated boots, then a salvo, then shots again, and, in between, cries. They were piercing yells which ensconced themselves in the labyrinth of the ear and remained there long after the yelling man was silenced forever. I had to be sick a second time. I lay on the bed, reduced to a bundle of misery. 'Now you are nothing but a bundle of misery,' I thought, and could not help grinning. Then it occurred to me that they had taken away my belt but not my tie. Above the bed was an iron hook for clothes, and I thought that really the most sensible thing to do would be to put an end to all this unpleasantness. The hook was placed very low, but I remembered having read in the papers that middle-aged clerks, on losing their jobs, have a predilection for hanging themselves on door-handles. That hook was anyhow no lower than a door-handle. I experimented a little but I found that it was a distinctly unpleasant procedure, and gave it up. After that

I felt an odd relief. I was happy to breathe again the stinking air of the cell : I suddenly felt very sleepy, and did not care about anything else. I slept soundly and peacefully until dawn.

When I awoke, I did not know where I was, and when I remembered I did not feel any the better for it. A few grimy rays of light filtered through the grimy window. Utter, bleak silence reigned. It is only in prisons that the air is so deaf.

It always requires resolution to get up in the morning. This morning there was nothing to get up for; no work awaited me, no mail, no duties. For the first time I experienced that curious feeling of freedom and irresponsibility which is one of the illusions of prison psychosis. I turned over on my wire mattress, pulled my legs up to my stomach to keep myself warm, and felt like a schoolboy playing truant. Then I dozed off again.

When I awoke, the light was still uncertain; a sound had awakened me. I listened; someone was singing : It sounded fairly near. The man who was singing must be in one of the isolation cells opposite. I sat up and felt my heart stand still : the man was singing the 'International'.

He was singing it out of tune, in a hoarse voice. He was obviously waiting for the other condemned men to join in. But no one joined in. He sang all alone in his cell, in the prison, and in the night.

I had read books about Nazi prisons and concentration camps. The singing of the 'International' as a political protest or as a last demonstration was frequently mentioned in them; but despite my profound respect for the German martyrs, such passages have always struck me as a little melodramatic and improbable. Now I myself was hearing a man who knew that he was going to die singing the 'International'. It was not melodramatic at all; the hoarse, unmelodious voice sounded wretched and pitiable. He repeated the refrain two or three times, dragging it out to make it last longer, to delay the moment when silence would return. I got up and posted myself by the door, and, my teeth chattering, stood to attention and raised my fist in the salute I had learned at meetings in Valencia and Madrid. I felt that in the adjoining cells the others were standing at their doors like myself, solemnly raising their fists.

He sang on and on. I could see him before me : the unshaven face, the broken nose, torture in his eyes.

He sang on and on. Didn't he realize that they would hear him outside and come and tear him to pieces?

He sang on and on. It was unbearable. We all loved him. But none of us joined in the singing.

*   *   *

About seven o'clock I heard the sound of shuffling feet and a great clatter and din in the corridor. I rushed to the spy-hole. Two warders were dragging along an enormous tub, about the size of a baby's bath, with a brown liquid in it. It was coffee. Two others were carrying a huge basket of bread.

The cell door opposite was opened, and I set eyes on the man who had been singing. At first all that I could see in the half-light was the bearded lower part of his face and a tattered shirt, stiff with congealed blood. He was standing in the corner of the cell farthest away from the door, his back pressed against the wall, his hand raised defensively in front of his face.

'Hombre,' said the warder who was carrying the ladle, an amiable old fellow, 'we're only bringing coffee. There's no beating here in prison.'

He filled the ladle with coffee and handed it to the singer, who put out both hands for it and gulped down its contents with terrifying avidity. He gulped and smacked his lips; it sounded just like a dog drinking. The four warders stood looking on. Then one of them handed him a hunk of bread from the basket. The man pressed the loaf against his shirt and gaped at the warders, the same hunted, half-crazed look still in his eyes. He panted. Then, obviously after a struggle, he asked :

'There won't be any more beating?'

'Not here in prison,' said the old warder.

As the door was being shut he pressed his outstretched hand against it and asked :

'When. . .?'

This was all he managed to get out.

The old warder shrugged his shoulders and closed the door.

The coffee and bread procession continued on its way from cell to cell of the row opposite. My field of vision was only wide enough to take in the singers' cell; but I could hear them coming along my row from the end of the corridor. Shortly before they reached my cell, a fifth warder came up with an armful of tin drinking vessels—old tinned-food containers and small petrol cans.

I was given my tin of coffee and my hunk of bread. But I had long since been considering whether it would not be better, now that I had already gone thirty-six hours without food and drink, to go on fasting and so weaken my powers of resistance as much as possible. While I had paced up and down, the screams of the tortured victims in the police station had continued to ring in my ears, almost as vividly as though I were the victim of an hallucination. If it comes to it, I thought, the weaker one is, the quicker one will lose consciousness.

So I poured the coffee down the W.C., and the bread too, after having broken it up into little pieces. In doing so, I had the impression that I was again taking an active part in the course of events, that I was putting up some sort of fight; and this thought had a calming effect. I crouched on my wire-mattress and tried to go to sleep.

I must have dozed off when the oily voice that I had heard in the morning woke me up again.

This time it came through the barred window from one of the courtyards through which I had wandered in search of Sir Peter. It read out twenty-five to thirty names. I could not count them exactly; the long, three-barrelled Spanish names confused me. This time all those whose names were called out had

to answer 'present', and if the answer did not come promptly, the
oily voice burst forth into a flood of abuse. Then it called out:
'All those from Cell No. 17.'
'All those from Cell 23.'
These were the nameless ones, who were shot and buried
anonymously.
The oily voice rose up twice more that night; once about
midnight—sixty names—once shortly before dawn. The last time
it came from a distant wing of the prison, an indistinct, faint
murmur; I could not keep count.
Then another day dawned.

It was Thursday now, not yet forty-eight hours since I had
been a free man, able to open doors with my own hand, comb
my hair, wash, blow my nose, and ring for the maid to bring a
drink.
About ten o'clock the singer was taken out of his cell.
This time no names were read out. A warder and two soldiers
approached the cell at a business-like pace. The warder swung
the door open and called out to its inmate: *'Valor, hombre'*
(Courage, man), then hurried on to the next cell; the soldier
seized the singer, bound his hands and led him away out of my
field of vision. Three more times I heard that *'Valor hombre'*
from varying distances in my corridor. Then all was silent again,
and I no longer had a companion opposite.
For two days I had eaten nothing, and during the previous
night I had slept little. After the *'Valor, hombres'*, I was pretty
well at the end of my tether.
I thought that there was really no point in going on with all
this, and wondered whether I should try that hook once more.
But the idea was not very tempting. I pulled myself up by the
bars of the window and in the cobwebby empty window frame
discovered a splinter of glass. It was as sharp as I needed for
my purpose. I was delighted with my discovery but thought it
would be better to wait until night.

The fact that I had made a decision which I regarded as final filled me with utter contentment. I became really cheerful, and the barometer rose at an astonishing rate. I called to memory, just by way of a test, the scene when the singer was led away, and the scenes in the police station. They now left me quite cold. I thought of friends and relatives, and found that I was not in the least bit moved. I was very proud of this Olympian frame of mind, and, true to the penny-dreadful, thought : nothing has power to move him who has done with life.

It was not until much later, in Seville, when I and a fellow-prisoner, both of us condemned to death, were discussing the various forms of fear, that I understood the secret of this magic metamorphosis; namely, that by coming to an apparent decision to take my life I had simply snatched for myself twelve untroubled hours. My state of Olympian calm was not, as I thought, the result of the decision itself, but of my having set a time limit of twelve hours. Up till now I had counted hourly on hearing the oily voice calling out my name; now, by a wishful inference, I took it for granted that the twelve hours respite which I had given myself would be respected by the outside world. This was why I was so cheerful.

I remained so until the afternoon, and then became even more cheerful when the door opened and the kindly old warder and an assistant dragged in a straw mattress. It was a dirty old mattress, and the straw sagged and stank, but when it had been laid over the iron springs and I had stretched myself out on it, I felt in all my aching joints how marvellously comforting it was compared with the iron springs which cut into the flesh. I grunted with satisfaction; the two warders looked on and grinned while I tried the mattress. They must have seen the same thing happen many times before, and been well aware of the enormous difference between a cell with a mattress and one without.

But a man is never satisfied; I wanted not only to have a soft, but a warm, bed to lie in. It was of course no use even dreaming of a blanket. So I tried to lie underneath the straw mattress and to use it as a blanket, but this arrangement was not satisfactory. Finally I hit upon an idea, With my splinter of glass I cut a long slit at the top end of the sacking and crept into it as I was, clothes, shoes, and all, crawling into it feet foremost, and then worming my way in bit by bit until only my head peeped forth from the slit. I felt I looked like an Egyptian mummy, and I promptly fell into a blissful sleep.

But the chain of lucky events was not yet over for that day. At five o'clock we were again brought a meal, although it was not yet twenty-four hours since we had last been fed. This time we were given a tin of corned beef per head and a hunk of bread. The meals in this prison, both as regards the times at which they were served and the menus, were highly original.

I decided that with my treasured splinter of glass in my pocket there was no longer any reason why I should go hungry, and I ate all my bread and half the corned beef at one sitting. The only thing lacking to make my state of contentment perfect was a glass of water. But after all, you can't expect to have everything in this life. I burrowed back into the straw, scratched myself for a while, and fell asleep again.

I was awakened at about ten o'clock in the evening by a noisy clatter and trampling of feet in the corridors. I was already an expert at diagnosing the prison noises, and realized at once that a new batch of prisoners was being brought in. The doors of a number of the adjoining cells, which the oily voice had freed of their inmates that morning, were opened and closed. Then my door too was opened.

A young man came in, or rather, was hurled in. The door closed behind him immediately. He stood leaning against the wall, his head drooping forwards. His shirt presented the appearance to which I was by now accustomed; it was torn and spattered with blood. The lacerated head, covered with contusions and clotted blood, and the crazed look in the eyes were also by now familiar. New to me, however, was a certain something about the face of this man, an anatomical irregularity which I could not at first make out; his lower jaw was dislocated and pushed out of its socket; it was set unbelievably askew in his face, as though it had been put on the wrong way round.

I crept out of the sacking and signed to him to sit down on the bed. He did not respond. I took him by the hand, led him the two paces over to the bedstead and helped him to sit down. He continued to stare straight ahead, felt his jaw with his hand and recoiled as though he had burned himself. In my embarrassment I handed some of the corned beef that had been left over, but he merely turned his head away. He could obviously neither eat nor speak. Perhaps not even think; but only suffer and be afraid and await the *coup de grace*.

I sat opposite him on the ground and held his hand. After a while he withdrew it. Fumbling slowly under his belt he produced two cigarette stumps. I took them and lit one of them; it was so short that I had to bend my head back horizontally to avoid burning my nose and lip. The human wreck grinned slightly out of the corners of his eyes, and signed to me to keep the other stump, that in any case he had no more use for it. I sat opposite him for a few minutes, not daring to say anything; any word of consolation seemed to me childish and somehow blasphemous. Only much later, in Seville, did I learn the simple facts that in such cases the content of what one says matters little, and the tone and gesture everything.

The silent *tête-à-tête* lasted only a few minutes; then my guest was taken away. He did not even turn his head when they bound his hands, on the threshold. They took him off to the left, towards the front gate. I did not hear a cell door close behind him. *Requiescat in pace.*

The Olympian calm had gone, and my misery had returned. The time had come for the splinter of glass to play its part, but I was far too apathetic to do anything at all. I didn't care two straws about anything; all I wanted was to creep into my cosy sacking and seek oblivion. At this moment I was really convinced that it was only out of laziness and apathy that I did not commit suicide. Of course I was deceiving myself again. The instinct of self-preservation, shrewd and indestructible, was playing tricks on me, presenting itself in various disguises. That morning it had donned the toga of Socrates, who, calm and collected, reaches out for the draught of hemlock. The mask had served its purpose; it had helped the mind through a crucial moment. Now it appeared in a new garb : that of St Simeon Stylites, who squats on his column and, blessed with indifference, lets the worms devour him.

*   *   *

Seville Prison

Why had I been put into a taboo cell? Why was I not allowed to join the others in the court and why were the prisoners in the court so afraid of looking in my direction? Was it indeed fear—or was it the embarrassment with which the healthy avert their gaze from the mortally ill?

And now at last I admitted to myself what had gradually been dawning on me from the start : I had been put in one of the condemned cells.

*   *   *

Tuesday, March 16th.[1]

Another jubilee. Five weeks since the day of my arrest.

If Franco had commuted the death sentence surely they would have let me know.

But it's doubtful whether they would also let me know of his refusal to commute. In that case, I suppose, one only hears that

---

[1] A. K. was able to keep a diary during part of the time he spent in Seville Prison, and to smuggle it out on his release.   (Ed.).

one's sentence is confirmed at the last moment.

After all, I was never told of the Malaga court-martial sentence.

Vaguely I recall precedents. Hauptmann, for example, the Lindbergh baby murderer, learned of the rejection of his appeal only twenty-four hours before going to the chair.

Don't know which is preferable. Perhaps it is preferable not to hear until the last moment.

The beastliest thing of all would be not to be informed of the commutation at all; to be left for months or years in uncertainty.

My mind has been following up this train of thought in all its permutations every day for the past week. Only wonder that my spirits are not much lower than they are. If ever I get out they'll hold up their hands and say how dreadful it must have been. And all the time I shall have a sly little feeling that, after all, the whole thing was not *so* bad as they imagine. Funny how elastic the limits of what is bearable are.

During the first few days I actually counted my shirt-buttons : reprieved—shot—reprieved—shot. Then I gave it up because an unfavourable result always terrified me.

The joke is one can't ever completely convince oneself that the whole thing is real and not a product of one's perverse imagination. Who does really believe in his own death? I remember Sir Peter telling me that one should disinfect the hypodermic syringe before committing suicide, or else one would get an abscess. I think there exists an almost mathematical relationship : one's disbelief in death grows in proportion to its nearness.

I don't believe that since the world began a human being has ever died *consciously*. When Socrates, surrounded by his pupils, reached out for the goblet of hemlock, he must have been at least half convinced that he was merely showing off. He must have felt like a ham actor and have secretly wondered at his disciples' taking him seriously. Of course he knew theoretically that the draining of the goblet would prove fatal; but he must have had a feeling that the whole thing was quite different from what his earnest and humourless pupils imagined it; that there was some clever dodge behind it all known only to himself.

Of course everyone knows that he must die some day. But to know is one thing, to believe another.

If it were not so, how could I feel as I write this that I am writing an abstract essay which personally doesn't concern me in the least?

True, at least once a day there is a short-circuit in my consciousness, and for minutes on end I behold reality in a shrill blaze of light, as though illumined by some psychical explosion.

Then no thoughts, no pills avail; only brute fear remains.

But it passes, everything passes; even the minute when one stands before the firing squad and the lead pierces its way through mouth and nose and eyes. And then it is all behind one.

So why get agitated, when it all passes?

Up to now I have kept myself under control and not written about these things. I must not do so again; it agitates me too much.

If only I could somehow get that black kitten into my cell.

Sunday, March 21st.

Rain, rain, the whole day. The courtyard is a swamp. Someone made a speech before Mass, but I could not understand it. Read and dreamed. I find myself sinking more and more into day-dreams—I lose myself for three or four hours on end, pacing up and down, up and down, in a half-dazed state.

Monday, March 22nd.

In the night my bed collapsed—I found myself on the floor and dreamed that I had been shot. Confirms the curious phenomenon that the fraction of a second between crash and waking is enough to construct *post factum* an entire story, leading up to the crash. The sound of the crash itself is only admitted to con-

8

sciousness *after* the story has been improvised—till then the bang must wait for admission on the threshold.

This execution dream was an exception—as a rule I now have mainly pleasant dreams. Never before have they been so beautiful. Often I laugh when dreaming, and my laughter wakes me up. Beautiful animals, Grecian scenery, also beautiful girls, but asexual. Am apparently developing an old-maid mentality; when reading I rejoice if the heroine remains chaste and the rules of decency are observed (formerly the contrary was true).

... Was reminded of my friend A.N., when he was being psycho-analysed. He seemed like a gored horse dragging itself across the bull ring, trailing its entrails behind it. Not a pleasant sight. Could not go to sleep again. Compared psycho-analysts to sewage-cleaners; the penetrating smell of their profession clings to them even in private life. In their eyes is always a look suggestive of spiritual sewage-cleaning.

Note with displeasure that I am becoming more and more malicious in my solitude. Maudlin and malicious.

Got three cigarettes from Angelito[1] at midday. Will try to smoke only one a day.

Planes again. Heinkels and Capronis, with white crosses on tail fins. Seven of them.

Evening barber came; offmowed beard with haircutting machine. Asked him why not with razor; he said razor-shaving costs money.

Wednesday, March 24th.

Smoked last cigarette at twelve. Once more got obsession of button-counting. In walking up and down take care always to tread in middle of flagstones, if, after pacing up and down five times, I haven't touched any of the edges, I shall be reprieved. Had often before attacks of such compulsions, hitherto always managed to fight them down; today for first time let myself go.

Six weeks today since arrest.

---

[1] Prison orderly. (Ed.)

Saturday, March 27th.

At midday offered to sell my watch to warder for hundred cigarettes. He refused. An hour later got my first letter from Dorothy and hundred pesetas.

I went half-insane with excitement. I embraced Angelito in presence of the warder and the prison secretary, who brought the letter.

Angelito grinned sourly all over his crinkled old woman's face, and was suddenly full of devotion and charm. He gave me ten cigarettes straight away as an advance against future tips; then they all marched off.

The letter is dated March the 8th—so it has taken twenty days to come.

It consists only of five or six cheering sentences, deliberately trivial in order to get past censor. It went in some mysterious way to the British Consul, Malaga, who passed it on to the military authorities, who forwarded it to the prison authorities. Whence it is obvious that my wife has so far been unable to discover my whereabouts. The last sentence says that I must without fail get a few words in my own handwriting to her via the consulate. From which I gather that she doesn't know whether I'm still alive or not.

Drummed on the door and asked whether I might answer the letter. The warder had obviously already received instructions on this point, for he said promptly I might not. I said I wanted to write only one sentence : that I am alive. He said it was impossible.

Then Angelito came to change the hundred peseta note into prison vouchers. He asked fawningly whether he could get me provisions from the canteen. With a lordly gesture I gave him pesetas, and told him spend it for me, telling him he could deduct two pesetas for himself straight away.

A magical transformation has come about in our relations. Hitherto I have felt myself entirely in Angelito's power and dependent on his moods; now he is a poor devil and I am a

Señor. It is a cheap satisfaction, but it gives me great pleasure.

With the evening soup he brought me a whole basketful of treasures. Cigarettes, matches, toothbrush, toothpaste, sardines in oil, sardines in tomato sauce, lettuce, vinegar, oil and salt in a special container, red paprika sausage, dried figs, cheese, Andalusian cakes, chocolate, tunnyfish in oil and four hard-boiled eggs. My bed was transformed into a delicatessen store. I poured my ration of lentils down the W.C. at one swoop, and devoured these luxuries in any order I fancied—chocolate and sardines, sausage and sweetmeats.

For the first time for six weeks I feel replete—sated, contented and tired.

If only I could get a word to Dorothy.

Tuesday, March 30th.

I fancy the *jefe*[1] only visited me because he had heard I have received some money. It is really curious to see how my prestige has risen overnight and how my own self-confidence has grown with it, since I have money.

Have sixty pesetas left; must begin to be careful.

Dreamed—for second time during imprisonment—that I was free. All rather colourless and disappointing.

Got J. S. Mill once more and made extracts whole day.

Sunday, April 4th.

Very bad day. Only a few hours' relief in sleeping and writing. My heart is giving me so much trouble that at times I feel as though I am suffocating. Whole day in bed in a kind of apathetic coma. The idea of getting up alarms me.

Have never been so wretched since Malaga.

During March forty-five men were shot.

During the first thirteen days of April there were no executions. During the night of April 13th to 14th seventeen men were

---

[1] Chief warder. (Ed.).

shot, in celebration of the anniversary of the proclamation of the Republic.

Two nights later, the night of Thursday, eight were shot. This was the first time I heard anything.

The proceedings were very subdued; that explains why I hadn't heard them before. But now I was warned and on the watch.

I had been told that the critical time was between midnight and two o'clock in the morning. For some days I stood from midnight until two o'clock with my ear pressed to the door of my cell.

During the first night of my vigil, the night of Wednesday, nothing happened.

During the second night. . . .

A feeling of nausea still comes over me when I remember that night.

I had gone to sleep, and I woke up shortly before midnight. In the black silence of the prison, charged with the nightmares of thirteen hundred sleeping men, I heard the murmured prayer of a priest and the ringing of the sanctus bell.

Then a cell door, the third to the left of mine, was opened, and a name was softly called out, '*Qué*'—What is the matter? —asked a sleepy voice, and the priest's voice grew clearer and the bell rang louder.

And now the drowsy man in his cell understood. At first he only groaned; then in a dull voice, he called for help : '*Socorro, socorro.*'

'*Hombre,* there's no help for you,' said the warder who accompanied the priest. He said this neither in a hostile nor in a friendly tone; it was simply a statement of fact. For a moment the man who was about to die was silent; the warder's quiet, sober manner puzzled him. Then he began to laugh. He kept slapping his knees with his hands, and his laughter was cackling and subdued, full of little gasps and hiccoughs. 'You are only pretending,' he said to the priest. 'I knew at once that you were only pretending.'

'*Hombre,* this is no pretence,' said the warder in the same dry tone as before.

They marched him off.

I heard him shouting outside. But the distant sound of the shots came only a few minutes later.

In the meantime the priest and the warder had opened the door of the next cell; it was No. 42, the second to my left. Again '*Qué?*' And again the prayer and the bell. This one sobbed and whimpered like a child. Then he cried out for his mother :
'*Madre, madre!*'

And again : '*Madre, madre!*'

'*Hombre,* why didn't you think of her before?' said the warder.

They marched him off.

They went on to the next cell. When my neighbour was called, he said nothing. Most probably he was already awake, and, like me, prepared. But when the priest had ended his prayer, he asked, as if of himself : 'Why must I die?' The priest answered in five words, uttered in a solemn voice but rather hurriedly : 'Faith, man. Death means release.'

They marched him off.

They came to my cell and the priest fumbled at the bolt. I could see him through the spy-hole. He was a short, black, greasy man.

'No, not this one,' said the warder.

They went on to the next cell. He, too, was prepared. He asked no questions. While the priest prayed, he began in a low voice to sing the 'Marseillaise.' But after a few bars his voice broke, and he too sobbed.

They marched him off.

And then there was silence again.

*   *   *

On the night of Tuesday seventeen were shot.
On Thursday night eight.
On Friday night nine.
On Saturday night thirteen.

I tore strips off my shirt and stuffed my ears with them so as not to hear anything during the night. It was no good. I cut my gums with a splinter of glass, and said they were bleeding, to obtain some iodized cotton wool. I stuffed the cotton wool in my ears; it was no good, either.

Our hearing became preternaturally sharp. We heard everything. On the nights of the executions we heard the telephone ring at ten o'clock. We heard the warder on duty answer it. We heard him repeating at short intervals: 'Ditto ... ditto ... ditto. ...' We knew it was someone at military headquarters reading out the list of those to be shot during the night. We knew that the warder wrote down a name before every 'ditto'. But we did not know whose names they were, and we did not know whether ours were among them.

The telephone always rang at ten. Then until midnight or one o'clock there was time to lie on one's bed and wait for the shrill sound of the night bell. It was the priest and the firing squad. They always arrived together.

Then began the opening of doors, the ringing of the sanctus bell, and praying of the priest, the cries for help and the shouts of *Madre*.

The steps came nearer down the corridor, receded, came nearer, receded. Now they were at the next cell; now they were in the other wing; now they were coming back. Clearest of all was always the priest's voice: 'Lord, have mercy on this man, Lord, forgive him his sins, Amen.' We lay on our beds and our teeth chattered.

On Tuesday night seventeen were shot.
On Thursday night eight were shot.
On Friday night nine were shot.
On Saturday night thirteen were shot.

Six days shalt thou labour, saith the Lord, and on the seventh day, the Sabbath, thou shalt do no manner of work.

On Sunday night three were shot.

*   *   *

Between the siesta and the evening meal the cell door flew open and freedom was hurled at me like a club; I was stunned, and stumbled back into life just as, had things taken another course, I should have stumbled into death.

As I stood in the corridor I shook from head to foot, over-powered by the same nervous trembling as on that night when someone outside my cell had called for help.

All that happened in the next few moments is dim in my memory, the contours blurred as though seen through a mist.

On the Governor's desk burned a naked electric bulb. All round it quivered an aura of light, like a street lamp flickering in a fog. In the Governor's chair sat a stranger. He was wearing a black suit, without a tie. He bowed with exaggerated formality.

'Señor,' the man in the black shirt said, 'I am taking you away from here.' Again I had to hold on to the table; I felt dizzy and feverish; eating after the long period of fasting had upset my system.

'Señor, said the man in the black shirt, 'I cannot tell you where I am taking you, but don't be afraid, we are *caballeros*.'

We went along the lighted corridor, I didn't know what they were going to do to me, I walked in my sleep. We went back to my cell. In a daze I packed my things. Again we walked along the corridor; the loose leaves of my diary dropped out of my pocket. The man in the black shirt helped me to pick them up. 'What have you got there, Señor?'

On the top lay my wife's letter stamped by the censor. 'Private letters,' I murmured. 'You can keep them, Señor, we are *caballeros*.' We went on down the corridor, opened another cell door.

I shook Byron and the Consumptive by the hand; they were both frightened. 'Where are they taking you?' 'I don't know,' I said. 'God bless you,' and the door fell to. We went on down the corridor and I shook hands—with Angelito and the other warders.

Then we were back in the office.

'Señor,' said the man in the black shirt, 'we are now going to another town, and if you are prepared to promise certain things I may then be able to take certain steps to procure your release.'

And he reached out for pen and ink. When I see pen and ink, I wake up at once.

'Señor,' I said. 'All this is so strange and so sudden. Who are you? What is this town you are taking me to? And what are these promises I am to make?'

'I would rather, Señor, not tell you my name. But we are *caballeros;* you can rely on us. We merely want you to promise that you will no longer meddle in the internal affairs of Spain. If you promise this, I may then be able to take certain steps to procure your release.'

'I have never meddled in the internal affairs of Spain.'

'You have engaged in a perifidious campaign against National Spain, Señor.'

'I wrote what I saw and what I thought about it. I have never meddled in the internal affairs of Spain.'

'I do not wish to argue with you, Señor. If you sign an undertaking that you will not meddle in the internal affairs of Spain, I may then be able to take certain steps to procure your release. But we are not going to force you, we are *caballeros.*'

I signed a declaration to the effect that I had no intention of meddling in the internal affairs of Spain. I wrote further that I had been treated correctly in the prison of Seville.

I learned later that my release was neither an act of mercy nor even a political gesture on the part of Franco. I was being exchanged against a prisoner of the Republican Government.

I learnt further details. The prisoner in question was a certain Señora Haya, who was being held as a hostage in Valencia. The *caballero* in the black shirt was her husband and one of Franco's most famous war pilots.[1]

Again we walked along the corridor, the man in the black shirt and I. A grille was pushed back, a key turned in the lock, a catch sprang back. Outside was the street.

Cars and donkey-carts were driving along the street. The people on the pavement walked here, there and everywhere in disorder, and not four abreast. A man leaned against the wall reading a newspaper. A child sat in the dust eating grapes.

In the garden outside the prison gates the guards stood about flirting with young girls. Girls with black hair; with roses stuck behind their ears. They wore skirts. They were quite wonderful girls.

'Señor,' said the man in the black shirt. 'If you have no objection, we will get into this car.'

We got into the car. At the back sat two discreet detectives. One plunged his hand into his pocket; I thought he was going to bring out the handcuffs, but it was a silver cigarette case.

We drove across the Guadalquivir; on the Guadalquivir there were ships. They trailed smoke behind them like loosened pigtails. They flew many-coloured flags. One blew its siren.

'Where are we going?' I asked.

'To another town,' answered the man in the black shirt.

On the café terraces sat people reading newspapers and drinking coloured drinks. There was a deafening noise in the streets. We almost ran into a tram. Then we drove along an avenue and the town was left behind. We drew up in an empty field and alighted. The *caballero* and the two detectives stood about irresolutely. For one last time I thought : now they're going to draw their revolvers and shoot you down; then I heard the hum-

---

[1] The *caballero* had been bluffing when he said he 'might be able to take steps to procure my release.' The agreement with regard to the exchange had been signed twenty-four hours before, through the mediation of the British authorities and the International Red Cross.

ming of an engine and a small monoplane appeared from behind the bushes and came rolling along towards us.

A mechanic jumped out and saluted. The man in the black shirt climbed into the pilot's seat; the mechanic helped me to get in beside him; the detectives each took a wing and pushed.

We rolled along right across the field; behind the bushes lay the aerodrome. A whole herd of steel saurians was grazing there with outspread wings.

The *caballero* pushed the joy-stick; the earth tipped over obliquely and sank into the depths at our feet.

We were in an improbably small machine, an open Baby Douglas, as delicate as a child's toy. We rose higher and higher, the horizon expanded, the city of Seville shrank. The *caballero* in the black shirt pursed his lips—I heard nothing, but could tell that he was whistling a tune to himself.

'Where are we going, Señor?' I yelled.

'To another town, Señor,' he yelled back.

We rose higher and higher. A mountain loomed towards us. White shreds of mist floated round us on all sides. The *caballero* in the black shirt pointed to the abyss below.

'All this is National Spain, Señor,' he yelled. 'Here everyone is happy now.'

'What?' I yelled.

'. . . happy,' he yelled, 'happy and free.'

'What?' I yelled.

'Free.'

IN BRITISH HANDS

By Krishna Nehru Hutheesing

TO write about my prison experiences or of those near and dear
to me, seems rather incongruous after all I have read and heard
at first hand of people who have suffered immeasurably in
prisons and concentration camps, especially during the last world
war. But ours was a very different kind of fight in more ways
than one.

I am told on the battlefield it's each man for himself. If one
does not kill the enemy, one will be killed by him. So one's mind
is gradually attuned to killing one's fellow human beings. Ours
was a non-violent battle. We wanted freedom from an alien rule
and though we outnumbered our rulers tremendously, we were
a crushed and frightened people. We had no will left to fight
and even if we had, we had no arms or equipment good enough
to cope with the armed might of the British Empire.

So Gandhiji came and preached the gospel of non-violence
to us as he considered that was the only way we could possibly
achieve freedom.

It was the year 1921 which brought things to a head. Gandhiji
seemed to cast a spell over all kinds of people and all over the
country one found a strange mixture of nationalism combined
with mysticism and a growing political fanaticism—yet though
thousands of us joined the civil disobedience movement and
pledged to free India from British rule, we were surprisingly free

from hatred against the British. Resentment and anger were there but only against the British Government—not the individual Englishman.

Throughout 1921 Congress workers were arrested all over India but it was only when the Prince of Wales visited India towards the end of that year, that mass arrests began. Prison was then an unknown place and courting arrest was a novelty. But soon it became a common, everyday affair for one's family to go in and out of prison and we got used to the inevitable police parties coming to recover fines imposed on those who were sentenced. As Gandhiji had instructed his followers not to pay fines or help the police in any manner, the latter usually collected whatever they considered the amount of the fine—from cars, fabulous carpets and furniture to smaller objects such as crystal vases and ashtrays. These were supposed to be auctioned and some of them were, but many things went to the homes of those who came to collect them.

Being imprisoned for political offences was not really a new thing in India when Mahatma Gandhi's Civil Disobedience movement started in 1921. Since the time of the partition of Bengal there had been spasmodic agitation and men had been going to prison in a fairly continuous stream for long terms without a trial. But the Civil Disobedience movement was unique in that Mahatma Gandhi appealed to the women of India in purdah and outside to join their menfolk in the struggle for freedom. Mahatma Gandhi stressed at every meeting that Independence could not be achieved if the women did not fight side by side with their men. The response was tremendous. Women, not necessarily in purdah but unused to going about in public, left the seclusion of their homes to join processions, attend meetings and court imprisonment.

Yet when our freedom struggle started in 1921 prison going was almost unknown and very few knew what was going on behind the grim gates that seemed to swallow the person who was arrested. Normally and in a vague fashion, we associated the prison inhabitants with desperate criminals. Prison meant a place of humiliation, isolation and a fear of the unknown. But frequent prison goings gradually accustomed us to the idea. Yet no amount of previous preparation really prepared any of us for what was forthcoming. One always entered the prison gates with a certain amount of excitement and tension.

The first time I was arrested it was for being a member of an illegal assembly. Together with several young men and girls we were taken to Malacca Jail (the name of the prison in my home town, Allahabad). We were young and excited at the prospect of being arrested which was a novel experience for us. When the iron gates closed and separated us from our comrades outside we had a queer sensation of aloneness and uncertainty. We stood together for a few minutes until the Matron—a short ugly looking woman—arrived and told us rather curtly to follow her, while the Gaoler took charge of the young men and we went to different sections of the prison. As soon as we reached the enclosure where we were to be kept, the Matron hustled and pushed four of us at a time into a cell and locked the door. Unused to being manhandled we were rather annoyed but curious to know where our other companions were locked up. We peered through the bars and failed to notice that there were three other women crouching in the cell. It was a long narrow barrack and as the interior was quite dark we had not seen anyone. Suddenly we heard a gurgling sound. All four of us turned round simultaneously and froze at what confronted us. The three women slowly moved towards us. At first we could not discern anything except the funny sounds they seemed to be making—chuckling, gurgling, squeaking. Gradually as they came out of the shadows we saw how horrible looking they were. One old woman was toothless with patches on her arms and face. The other had no nose and also had pink patches on her face and semi-naked breast. The third whose face was not marked had the most cruel expression I have ever seen on anyone's face. She it was who silently approached us while the others made peculiar sounds, and held out her arms towards us with an evil grin. It was then we noticed she had three fingers on one hand and only a thumb on the other and the same patches on her arms. I was the youngest of our group and apart from being horribly frightened I had no idea what the patches and loss of fingers and nose meant. But two of our companions guessed and whispered—'They are lepers.' Half dead with fright and sickened by their appearance we took a few steps backward only to find ourselves glued to the iron door. At first we were too stunned to know what to do and just clutched each other round the waist for moral support—steadily the three women came nearer and nearer so that we were able to distinguish even the sores on their bodies. We held our breath and waited, unable to tell them to go back and leave us alone as we seemed to have lost the power of speech through fear. The woman who had lost her fingers suddenly advanced quickly towards one of my friends and was about to stroke her arm when the girl screamed and broke the tension. All of us started screaming with all our might and this somewhat upset the leper women who stood rooted to the spot as if fascinated by our behaviour. Our fellow prisoners in other cells came to their bars and shouted asking us what was wrong but we just screamed until the wardresses came running and the head wardress opened our door. Before she could enter or ask questions we knocked her down and still screaming rushed out into the yard. One of the girls fainted, the rest of us just wept hysterically clutching at the bars of the other cells inside which our friends were locked.

The Matron had been sent for and came in a towering rage. She told us to get back into the cell but we refused. She hit us with a baton but we did not move. Our screams and the Matron's abuses were heard in the men's yard as only a wall separated us, and thinking we were being ill treated, they started shouting for the Superintendent and Gaoler. As we were the first political prisoners in that gaol the Matron did not quite know how harsh she could be, so she waited and kept on hurling abuses at us. Soon the Superintendent, an Englishman, came and asked the Matron what had happened. Of course she merely said nothing had happened; we had just started screaming until the cell was opened, then knocked over a wardress and come out, refusing to go back.

Sternly, the Superintendent asked us what we meant by such behaviour as we ourselves had courted imprisonment. Too frightened and hysterical to be able to speak coherently we just pointed to the cell. At first the Superintendent could not understand, nor could he see anything as the women had crept back into the darkest corner, but then he stepped in and ordered them to come forward. They remained crouching until one of the wardresses went in and dragged them out. We saw the look of horror on the Superintendent's face which turned to livid rage as he asked the Matron why she had put us young girls into that particular cell. Cringing before him she replied : 'Sir, I thought I would teach these troublemakers a lesson once and for all and then you would not be bothered with them again.' Still very angry but not wishing to scold her before us he ordered us to be put into the same cell as our other companions who were all much older, and then hastily left the yard telling the matron to follow him. Apparently he not only gave her a dressing down but got in touch with the magistrate who had ordered our arrest. After a couple of hours we were all released—no reasons were given. Altogether we were in prison for six hours! But the experience had shattered our nerves and somewhat dampened our patriotism for a short while. Though our first term in prison ended rather suddenly it gave us an inkling of what to expect in future if we got arrested.

The second time I was arrested was when my father, who had been released, was lying very ill at home. He had repeatedly hinted that he hoped I would not do anything deliberate which might lead to arrest as he wanted me with him. My brother Jawahar and his wife were both in prison and I also had no desire to court imprisonment during that time. One day, having obtained permission to attend the trial of some of my colleagues in the Youth League of which I was then the Secretary, I went with a cousin of mine, Shyamkumari, and two other friends to the prison where we had been kept a few hours; in those days most trials took place inside prisons. Our colleagues were sentenced to varied terms of imprisonment and when the so-called trial was over the magistrate left the room. We said goodbye to our friends and waited until they had been ushered inside; then we turned to the outer gate to be let out. But instead an Inspector of Police who had been at the trial confronted us with a warrant of arrest. We were completely taken aback as we had not been actively participating in the movement for quite some time; but when we questioned the Inspector he merely shrugged his shoulders and said it was because we had engaged in unlawful activities some time ago. My cousin Shyamkumari was a lawyer and took no part in active politics except for joining in a procession now and again as thousands of others did. She tried to argue with the Inspector but it was no use. He said the magistrate had made out the warrant; his duty was to serve it, which he had done. The magistrate who had sentenced our friends and signed the warrant for our arrest came back after fifteen minutes. We had some sort of a mock trial and were all four sentenced to one month's imprisonment or 100 Rupees fine.

So once again we were taken inside the gaol. The old Matron was no longer there; instead there was another who resembled a procuress and was fat and evil looking. It was winter and our cell very cold, with vermin crawling all over the place. We had nothing with us and were told to send for some clothes and bedding from home; we did this by asking those who always gathered outside the gaol on such occasions to inform our parents.

I was terribly unhappy wondering what my father would think and hoping he would understand that I had not done anything deliberately to get arrested. My cousin and I were alone in a cell. After about an hour our bedding and a few clothes arrived from home and we spent some time trying to brush all the crawling insects out of the cell; we then made our beds on the cold stone floor. We talked for a while, then gradually fell asleep only to be woken up hours later by the sound of voices, clanging chains and gates opening. We were wondering what was going on when we saw a small group coming towards our cell. The Matron curtly told us to get up and fold our bedding as we were being released. Our fines had been paid, not by our parents but by anonymous friends, who refused to admit to this for many years. This time we spent exactly twelve hours in prison.

In February, 1931, father died. He had been very close to me and without him I felt the world crumbling at my feet. For a couple of months I behaved rather badly and was inconsolable, not giving a thought to my mother, brother or sister who were equally stricken. Then my brother sent me away to spend some time with a cousin of mine, R. K. Nehru (now our Secretary General), and his wife. They were very kind and after spending a month with them I returned home and threw myself into politics. My sister, Vijayalakshmi, who had until then not taken a very active part in the freedom movement, did likewise.

In December 1931 several women workers including my sister and myself, were served with notices forbidding us to take part in meetings or processions for the period of one month. My brother, Jawahar had been arrested a few days before at a way-side station a few miles from Allahabad, en route to Bombay. Nevertheless, we had decided to bide our time but on the 26th December one of the largest meetings was held in our home town. My mother presided over it and gave a fiery speech but before the meeting could terminate properly there was a lathi charge and the meeting had to break up. Many were arrested on the spot but as my mother was among the injured the police left us to look after her. The next morning at 9 o'clock a police car arrived with an inspector and several policemen and informed me that I was under arrest. A similar warrant was served on my sister at her house as well as on some of our cousins and co-workers. It was hard to say goodbye to my mother who stood in the porch looking so frail and lonely in the great big house. She waved, smiling bravely, as the car took me away.

I accompanied the Inspector to the prison where I had been twice before. My sister and the other women were already there and I felt a little more reassured at seeing them. We were hustled into the now familiar yard after the formalities of weighing us and so forth had been completed. We were kept three weeks under trial, which was not usual in previous years. Each morning during this time, the Superintendent, an Englishman, who had been badly shell-shocked during the war, came on his rounds and inspected the prisoners to see that none was missing. We had to assemble in our yard and one day a friend of mine and I were late in appearing from our cell. As soon as he saw us he shouted : 'Hurry up, hurry up, you there. I can't wait all day for you. Don't you know a tennis tournament is on which I want to see, and I am held up here in this most unpleasant place because of you difficult women who should be looking after your homes, your husbands and children instead of trying to be heroines.' I retorted : 'We find this filthy prison even more annoying than you do, Col. X. And as for missing the tennis tournament, I too am a tennis fan. Why should you not miss part of it one day when we are missing it every day?' The Superintendent became so livid that we thought he would have a stroke, but curbing his anger he stamped out of the yard. It was only later I discovered that for my insubordination I was not to be allowed to see my mother for a week, though while under trial we were permitted daily interviews of twenty minutes in the prison office.

The first few days were a novel experience, but each night was a nightmare. All sorts of insects crawled around us and over our blankets. We found them in our bedding in the morning. For some unknown reason they never crawled over our faces yet the dread that they might do so kept us awake half the night. It gave one an awful feeling imagining some slimy insect creeping up one's arms or legs. A couple of girls with us did experience this so we used to have a general clean up of the cell before it became dark. It helped a little.

After three long weeks we were tried and sentenced to one year's rigorous imprisonment plus 1500 Rupees fine for my sister and myself, in lieu of which, we could do another three months each. The others got varying sentences from three months to a year. After four days we were woken up at 11 p.m. and told to pack as we were being transferred to another jail. We discovered that we were being taken to the Lucknow Central Prison; we remained there a little over eleven and a half months—getting ten days for good conduct!

It was a bitterly cold morning when we arrived at our destination and the prison looked enormous with its very high walls and sinister appearance. My heart sank but I was determined not to be cowed.

We had come to prison of our own accord though quite a few had been arrested for no special offence other than that they happened to be in a procession or at a meeting. However, there was no question of any of us trying to escape. If any one wanted to get out of prison, all he or she had to do was to express regret for his or her action and give an undertaking that they would refrain from political activity in future. But this never happened.

We were kept in a larger barrack—ten of us. We were locked up at 5.30 p.m. and the cell was opened at 5.30 a.m. every morning. All day we were allowed to do what we liked and wander around the yard which kept us separated from the rest of the wards. Being 'A' class prisoners we were allowed an interview every fortnight with near relations, but as my father had died and my brother and brother-in-law, Ranjit Pandit were in prison, only our mother and sometimes Kamala, Jawahar's wife, could come to see us. Often nobody came, and as interview days were highlights in the monotonous routine of our daily life we spent the entire day feeling depressed.

The Lucknow Central Prison was a jail for juvenile convicts —ranging from twelve or thirteen to twenty-one years. The wardresses were 'lifers' hardened by long terms in various prisons, vicious, cruel and immune to any finer feelings for the young girls who had come there and whom they bullied and thrashed merci- lessly. But it was not only the young convicts whom they perse- cuted but also some of the women political prisoners who were in 'B' and 'C' classes and did not have the privileges of 'A' class pris- oners. It was thought that we who were given 'A' class would be treated better and in some ways we were—but on the whole it was only our leaders who really got special treatment; apart from the advantage of interviews and letters, we had to eat the gaol food and were often insulted and abused by the wardresses.

One of them asked me soon after our arrival in Lucknow jail, 'Are you in for murder? Poisoning? Arson? Theft?' When I said, 'No,' to everything she said, 'Gandhi?' and said 'Yes'. With a look of utter disgust she walked away as if I wasn't worth bothering about.

We were crowded together, our beds about four feet from each other, and everyone wanted to do different things such as read- ing aloud, humming a song or chanting verses from the Gita or Ramayana. The utter lack of privacy became unendurable as the time went by. There were the same petty irritations and annoyances day in and day out and no means of escaping to a quiet corner by oneself. We had to bathe in public—wash our clothes in public and put up with taunts from the matron as well as the wardresses if we showed any signs of being finicky regard- ing cleanliness or food. The nervous strain kept us tense and we often got involved in petty quarrels with each other.

Today time is a luxury for most of us but in those days it was a burden. All we could see of the outside world was the sky and the tops of a few trees. After several months, when it started to get warm, we were no longer locked up in our barracks but allowed to sleep in the yard. I had always loved the sunset and the clouds chasing each other across the blue sky, and the first rains followed by the fresh smell of the earth. But in prison, with time hanging endlessly on our hands, all this became even more important. Lying under the open sky looking for the various constellations and watching the twilight turn to night, everything took on a new aspect and one seemed closer to nature than before. But we never saw the sunrise or sunset and only the blazing sun emerged over our high walls. What we missed most were the vivid colours of nature, of trees and flowers and greenery. All we saw were the drab grey walls and the dirtily clad convicts; soon our own spotless white handspun saris turned to cream then light grey and then a darker grey. We were only allowed six saris and not being used to washing anything, least of all such thick materials, I'm afraid we did not make a very good job of it.

As the national movement gained momentum outside, restrictions inside became more and more severe and stricter rules were enforced. Newspapers were not allowed but nevertheless bits of news trickled through. Every effort was made to keep political prisoners and convicts apart. This was more easily done in the men's prison as certain gaols were reserved only for politicals. But it was not so easy in women's gaols as there were not such large numbers of us. Living as we had done, until the civil disobedience movement brought us out of our life of comfort, in a world where we knew little of what happened to convicts, it was a shock to find out, as we gradually did, what the realities of prison life were in those times. Violence, as well as graft and corruption, was the order of the day. Food was terrible; the staff were underpaid and incompetent, so they made use of every opportunity to extort money from the poor prisoners or their relatives. The administration, as laid down in the gaol manual, had nothing whatever to do with reforming a prisoner or teaching him a useful trade so that he could, when released, earn an honest living. To us it seemed the main object of prison was to harass a convict and break his spirits.

The majority of politicals suffered the same treatment as the convicts, but being there for a different reason, they refused to submit to their gaolers or be exploited. For this reason they were unpopular with the staff who invented all sorts of devices to irritate them. Sometimes, when they could not stand the treatment they became aggressive but if any of them committed a breach of discipline they were severely punished by being flogged or given solitary confinement.

European and Eurasian prisoners of both sexes were treated better. One did not grudge them the few privileges they obtained but it was painful and at times shocking to see the complete absence of human standards in the behaviour of the gaol officials towards men and women alike.

What saddened me most was that so many young girls were sentenced to long terms of imprisonment. There were quite a few who were bright-eyed, pretty and very innocent looking. It seemed inconceivable that they had committed the crimes for which they had been gaoled. Even if they had been driven to such acts they should have been kept away from the older and hardened criminals.

One of the young convicts was called Bachuli. She was a fair, grey-eyed girl, plump and not quite five feet tall, with coarse matted hair down to her shoulders. Yet, in spite of her rough clothes and none too clean appearance, she made a pretty picture when I saw her for the first time against the grim prison walls trying to learn to crochet. She looked so very young and had such an innocent expression that I wondered why she was in gaol, or what great offence this mere child could have committed. When I walked up to her she was humming a song, one of those sad haunting melodies one hears in the mountains of northern India.

'What is your name?' I asked her.

She looked at me suspiciously and asked in her turn very gently and hesitatingly, 'Who are you and how did you get in here?'

'I am a prisoner too,' I replied, and she burst out laughing.

'What are you in for?' she asked again. I told her I was a political prisoner and though she nodded her head wisely, I think she only vaguely understood what it meant. Anyway she decided I was trying to be friendly, and satisfied that I was not a gaol official, she told me her name. Shyly she looked up at me with a very lovely smile and then with a sigh resumed her work.

'Why are you here, Bachuli?' I asked. A pair of large, frank eyes looked straight into mine and she said simply, 'For murder!'

'For murder?' I asked incredulously, and she nodded her head to confirm it. I could hardly believe my eyes or ears. This child in her teens could not possibly have murdered anyone. There must be some mistake.

'Bachuli, why did you have to murder someone?' I asked. 'You are so young. Perhaps you did not know what you were doing. It may have been an accident.' She raised her head slowly and looked at me again. The laughter had gone from her eyes and in its place came a look of fear and hatred which hardened her usually soft expression.

This is her story:

'It was my husband I murdered,' she said slowly. 'He was very cruel to me and beat me and locked me up very often. He also made me starve and though there was always enough to eat in the house, he would take my share away from me and give me very little of it, eating the rest himself or throwing it away. Every now and then he would invent some new way of causing me pain, though I tried hard to please him. He was very good-looking and when I married him I was only fourteen years old, but I liked him and I vowed to the Gods and Goddesses that I would be a good wife to him, serve and obey him, as my mother had told me to, and feed him well. But a few months after our marriage he suddenly started being cruel, and it gave him pleasure to see me being afraid of him. He told me that he teased me because it amused him, and I was terribly frightened.

'For nearly a year I suffered. My husband would not let me go back to my parents, though I begged him to do so. Each day I became more and more unhappy. In spite of all this ill-treatment, I tried to make him like me, but nothing I could do would help or please him. One morning he gave me a thrashing because I had not washed a coat of his that he wanted to wear, and after the thrashing he went out, leaving me in agony. Some hours later he returned, dressed in new clothes with a bright red silk handkerchief around his neck. I was doing some work and did not turn round when he entered. So he called to me, "Come here, you little idiot, and admire my new clothes. Do I not look handsome in them?"

'I did not reply, but looked at my own clothes, which were dirty and torn.

' "Speak up, can't you?" he shouted. "Or are you jealous of my new clothes?"

'I still remained quiet. So he came up to me and slapped my face twice, holding my wrist so that it hurt me terribly.

' "Let go of me," I cried, "or I shall kill you one of these days. Why should I admire your clothes when you eat all day long and starve me? Why? . . ." and before I could finish or say any more, he took his stick and, abusing and cursing me, he hit me again and again till I nearly fainted, and then he flung me aside. "Now try and kill me," he said, and, throwing away his stick, he calmly lay down and soon fell off to sleep.

'After some hours had elasped I tried to move, but all my body ached and I lay down again. Suddenly I saw my husband fast asleep in a corner. He had taken off his new clothes and hung them up, but the new silk handkerchief was still round his neck. As I looked at him I hated him and all of a sudden I felt I should kill him and be done with him. But how? I looked around and found nothing with which I could hit him. Then my glance fell on the bright, red handkerchief. I do not know how it happened but I was up in no time, tying the handkerchief tighter and tighter round my husband's neck. He woke up at the first pressure, struggled and tried to shout, but I just went on tightening the handkerchief till his eyes nearly came out of their sockets and then he went limp. I let go, and, being utterly exhausted, I fell back in a daze, half expecting my husband to get up and give me another thrashing. But he did not and I lay there beside him unable to move.

'That is how someone found us the next morning. He discovered my husband was dead and sent for the police and ran hither and thither telling all our neighbours. I was still dazed, unable to believe that I had really killed my husband.

'No one came near me till a policeman arrived and I was taken away to prison. After my trial I was sent to this prison and so here I am. I was too young to be hanged and women do not usually get a death sentence. I got life imprisonment. That is all.'

I had listened to this strange tale in silence with my eyes on Bachuli's face. I still could not believe what she had told me, and yet it must be true, as she was in prison.

As though she had told me just a story, Bachuli resumed her work. She was not curious to know what effect her story had had on me. To her it was an incident which in her innocence and simplicity she believed the fates had willed. She submitted to her life in prison as a matter of course, something which could not be averted, and so why worry?

One night when all was deadly quiet and everyone was asleep, the girl next to me woke me up. 'Listen,' she said, 'do you hear anything?'

I listened, and every now and then I heard a jingle of bells, faint in the distance. 'What is it?' I asked.

'I do not know,' said my friend, 'but it gives me a creepy feeling. There was a dancing-girl here who was sentenced to death and hanged. Maybe it is her ghost that haunts the prison.'

I shivered. I had no desire to see ghosts in prison, or elsewhere, but I pretended not to bother about it. I told my friend not to imagine things and that it was not possible to have ghosts strolling around a prison. Even they, I was sure, would draw the line at that. My friend did not think it at all funny and snubbed me accordingly. The sound became more and more distant and soon we could not hear it at all.

The next night we again woke up to hear the same sound and

we did not feel at all happy about it. We lay awake trying to figure out what it could be but were not successful. For three nights this went on, and on the fourth night, the noise came nearer and was much louder. With tense nerves we waited, and soon we saw a figure all in black turn round the corner of one of the barracks; the jingling sound came from it. For a few seconds we could not make out what it was; then, like a flash, it dawned on us that it must be a wardress. Our relief was so great that we nearly shouted with joy. The wardress was supposed to go round the whole women's jail every night; but being very lazy and thinking it not necessary to come into the political prisoners' yard, she had avoided our part of the prison. The jingling sound came from an enormous bunch of keys hanging at her waist.

Next morning we decided to tell the others and have a good laugh at our own expense. As soon as we started our story, we saw them looking at each other very meaningly. We questioned them, and after much persuasion they told us that they had each heard the bells and had come to the same conclusion as we had about the ghost, but had not said anything for fear of alarming us.

But every episode in gaol was not one over which we could laugh. The treatment meted out to the young girl-convicts made one's blood boil and yet we were powerless to help them. The wardresses were of the worst type and were generally rude and insulting to all the politicals. It was difficult enough to control one's temper when they spoke rudely to us but it was far worse to see and hear them abusing the other convicts for some petty thing.

One of the young political prisoners in our yard was a vivacious, plump girl of about nineteen. When she arrived with a new batch of prisoners her good spirits were a help to us all. Along with the other girls she hummed national songs, sometimes a love song or chatted gaily to all and sundry. Her name was Alaka. She had wanted to continue her studies but her parents arranged a match for her. At first she resented the idea but when she saw her fiancé, a slim handsome young man, who met her frightened gaze with a frank disarming smile, she was completely won over by him. They were married and for a year were wonderfully happy. Then the entire country was shaken up by the Civil Disobedience Movement and both Alaka and her husband Jayant joined it. One day the police came and arrested Jayant and after that Alaka threw herself more whole-heartedly into her work until, along with her co-workers she too was arrested. Soon after Jayant's arrest Alaka discovered she was pregnant but because with the excitement all round she paid little attention to the fact. Once in jail she decided to keep her secret as ordinarily, pregnant women politicals were not imprisoned. One day scanning a newspaper that had been smuggled in Alaka saw her husband's name splashed across the front page; he was supposed to have been involved in a Bomb Case. Aghast at what she read, when she grasped the full implication of such a charge she came to me and tearfully asked what she should do. I told her there was nothing she could possibly do while a prisoner herself but she said she would speak to the Superintendent and beg him to at least have her transferred to somewhere near her husband's gaol. When the Superintendent came on his rounds the next day she spoke to him and said she had heard this news from one of the other women who had had an interview. She begged him to have her sent to the prison where her husband was kept. The Superintendent was a kindly man but lived in mortal fear of annoying his English superiors. A month passed and suddenly Alaka was informed she was to be transferred. She was overjoyed but none of us were very pleased. She was very young and we were loath to let her go alone to an unknown destination. Together we sent a petition to the Superintendent to allow one of the older women to accompany Alaka wherever she was being sent. But the request was curtly turned down.

Next morning as Alaka gaily said goodbye to all of us she

whispered to me and those nearby that she was pregnant. 'I am not worried at all,' she said, 'because may be like Lord Krishna my son will be born in gaol,' and before we could recover from our surprise she had been escorted out of the yard. The rest of us got together trying to work out what to do to prevent Alaka going alone in this condition. The oldest among us begged an interview with the Superintendent immediately, hoping to see him before Alaka had gone through the usual formality of transfer. But the Superintendent was busy and Alaka was taken away.

As the slow passenger train crawled along Alaka began to feel somewhat uneasy. She knew that part of the country and the stations they passed were unfamiliar ones. So she enquired of the two wardresses accompanying her if they were going to Ferozepore. At first they refused to reply but when she kept on insisting one of them told her reluctantly that they were going to another town. Alarmed and somewhat frightened Alaka cried : 'But that is not where I am supposed to go. You have made a mistake, you fools, stop the train, take me back,' and she ran towards the door of the compartment to pull the alarm signal. A wardress grabbed her by the arm and when she resisted, the other slapped her hard across her face several times. Stunned by the impact Alaka cowered down in a corner and did not move until she reached her desitination.

Wholly at a loss as to what to do, alone and friendless, she got down wearily from the train and into a black maria which was waiting to take her to the new gaol. As they approached it Alaka saw that though it was a smaller prison it looked very sinister— only the thought that perhaps Jayant too was there revived her sinking spirits.

It was a pitch black night when Alaka was ushered into a solitary cell by the Matron. As she was being locked up she asked where the other women political prisoners were and was told there were no others. Alaka grabbed the Matron's sleeve and asked if she could see the Superintendent in the morning. The

Matron held up the lantern to look at Alaka's face and for the first time Alaka saw hers, and recoiled with horror at the sight that met her gaze. The woman's face was deeply pock-marked, scarred and evil looking with bloodshot eyes. With a leering smile that froze one's blood she looked at Alaka appraisingly, 'No, my pretty one, you cannot see the Superintendent Sahib to-morrow,' she said. 'Who do you think you are that the Superintendent Sahib can see you whenever you wish? You will see him when he has time. Meanwhile, if you behave and listen to me you will be happy here for I like young girls like you. Most of the time we get old hags here and I'm sick of them. If you give me any trouble, my fresh young rose-bud, I'll break every bone in your body.'

Horrified by what she saw and heard Alaka backed away into a corner of the cell. Seeing her do this the Matron told the wardresses to go away; she opened the cell and entered it. Coming close up to Alaka, she at first let her eyes stray over her from head to foot, taking in the minutest details of the girl's youthfulness and smooth skin. She put out her hand to stroke Alaka, who half dead with fright, shrank as far back as she could. Seeing her really scared, the Matron cackled and hobbled away.

For a week Alaka was left severely alone. Then she was summoned to the Superintendent's office. 'Where is my husband?' asked Alaka. 'I was transferred here so that I could have an interview with him.' Instead of replying to her question the Superintendent asked her to sit down and pointing to three men sitting a little farther away said, 'Your husband has been involved in a Bomb Case while he pretended to be carrying on non-violent activities. These gentlemen are here to ask you a few questions about your husband's activities. Who were his close associates, where did he work and so on. He has been questioned but denies he had had anything to do with terrorist activities as he is a disciple of Gandhi's. But we know he is lying. If you tell us the truth about his secret work you will be released. If you don't he will be hanged for treason and you will be kept here.'

'But what is there to tell,' Alaka cried. 'I know my husband is wrongly accused. He has always been a Satyagrahi and was doing what thousands of Congressmen did. He hated violence or bloodshed. How can you accuse him of such a crime? I was told I was being transferred in order to see him. If he is not here, send me back. I cannot tell you anything as there is nothing to tell and I certainly will not give you the names of our friends.'

Calmly the Superintendent turned towards the Matron and said: 'Use your persuasive methods on her, Matron, and make her talk.'

Completely bewildered Alaka allowed herself to be led back to the cell. She felt weak physically, her mind was dazed and her thoughts jumbled and confused. What did they want her to confess when there was nothing to confess? And Jayant—where was he, why were they being kept apart so cruelly? Suddenly she seemed heavy with child and longed for the affectionate companionship of those she had left in the other prison.

Alaka lay inert in her cell as though she had been drained of all her strength; she did not touch the food on her tin plate. Evening came and the prisoners were all locked up. The hum and noise that had continued in the yard suddenly ceased and silence reigned over the prison and its inmates. Alaka did not know how long she had been lying there when she heard the outer gate opening and chains clanging; hopefully, she thought it might be another political prisoner. Footsteps came nearer and the key turned in the lock of her cell. Hoping some good news was being brought to her Alaka got up as the Matron entered, locking the door behind her. 'Don't be afraid,' she said, 'come closer child for I want to keep you company. Frightened and nervous Alaka shrank away, but found herself in the vicelike grip of the Matron who pulled her forwards pressing her own fat ungainly body against Alaka's. Not daring to speak, Alaka did not move while the Matron opened her blouse and slipped her coarse hand over Alaka's shoulder over her breasts and down her body, all the while muttering to herself whilst clutching Alaka as close as she could with one arm.

Alaka stood it as long as she could then nauseated, tore herself away. 'Don't touch me you wicked woman. How can you be so evil? I'm not one of your wretched convicts. Go away from me. Get out or I shall report you to the Superintendent tomorrow.'

'You will, will you,' said the Matron, leering at her. 'But who will take your message except me? And I, dear child, have fallen in love with you. I want you and if you don't submit to my embraces I can use force.'

Gasping for breath Alaka stammered, 'Please don't touch me. I'm going to have a baby—don't come near me.'

Taken aback the Matron tore Alaka's sari off and saw her enlarged stomach which she apparently had not noticed— 'Curse you, oh Curse you! I thought I'd get some pleasure out of you. Well, take that and that' she screamed hysterically kicking Alaka wherever she could. Then lifting her cane she hit Alaka's face and body relentlessly till the girl collapsed in a dead faint.

When the Matron realized that Alaka was unconscious she shouted to a wardress to bring a bucket of water which she flung on Alaka's face and left her. For hours Alaka lay semi-conscious only to wake up with a terrible spasm of pain which seemed to tear her body to pieces. Again and again the pains came on till unable to bear any more she gave a piercing yell and drifted into complete unconsciousness. How long she remained that way she did not know but when she regained consciousness she realized that her baby had been born. Aching in every limb she saw a tiny creature lying near her with the umbilical cord still binding it to its mother. Frantically she looked for something to sever the cord with but there was nothing. Then her eyes fell on her glass bangles. Breaking them she cut the cord after what seemed an eternity, for the little bit of glass would not cut quickly. This done, she picked up the baby and cleaned it as well as she could

with her sari and held it to her. But the baby made no sounds
nor did it move. Strangely frightened, she patted it on the back
as she had seen the midwife do when her younger sisters and
brothers were born, but no sound came. Slowly realization
dawned on her—her baby was dead. Holding it to her as closely
as she could, she sat surrounded by blood—tearless, dazed and
worn out with fatigue and the horrible experience she had under-
gone. This is how Alaka was found next morning in a delirious
state with high fever, still holding on to her dead child. She was
brought back to our prison hospital and as I was her friend, I
and an elderly cousin of mine were allowed to visit her. Perturbed by her condition and having gathered from her talks with
us what had happened, the Superintendent must have informed
the Government and her parents were asked to come and take
her away. A week later she died.

Though personally I did not suffer as many others did during
imprisonment, I found the lack of human touch, the insolent
way we were talked to and the oppressive atmosphere of the
place, at times became unbearable. The very air seemed different
from that of the outer world. It was full of menace, violence,
meanness and graft and there was always cursing on one side
and cringing on the other. A person who was at all sensitive was
in a state of continuous tension with their nerves on edge. Trivial
matters would be upsetting and a piece of bad news in a letter
or in a newspaper which had been smuggled in, made one ill
with anxiety. Those outside found relief in action and in various
activities and so gained some sort of equilibrium of mind and
body. In prison there was no outlet. Bottled up and repressed a
one-sided and perhaps rather distorted view of happenings, was
inevitable.

It was after a spell in prison that one began to appreciate the
value of the little things of life which one had before perhaps
taken for granted. Very few belongings were allowed and they
could not easily be added to, so one clung to them and gathered
odd bits and pieces which in the world outside one would hardly

notice. The sense of property strangely enough does not leave one even when there is nothing worth while to own.

At times a great longing would overtake me for the sight of a loved face or the sound of a familiar voice. One also missed bodily comforts and pleasant surroundings, but most of all one missed interesting conversation, children's voices and the sights of nature. Prisoners, especially those with long terms, suffer most from emotional starvation. As political prisoners in India, on the whole, we were treated far better than political prisoners in other parts of the world. Our leaders, unlike great men of other countries, were treated with some deference, if not politeness, and this perhaps is one of the reasons that we bear no ill-will or bitterness towards the British today. It used to stagger me when I heard from friends or read about the hatred that individuals of one country had for another—because we never felt it. Different countries with different traditions may also account for certain reactions. Since ours had a tradition of tolerance and resignation, we took all that came our way without any feeling of hatred creeping into our system.

The long days in prison were fraught with the cruelty of separation and frustration and one wondered what truth there was in the saying that 'life's rich gifts follow frustration, cruelty and separation!' Suffering may be necessary to enable one to think cleanly, yet an excess of it could and has warped the brain. The sort of prison life we led encouraged introspection.

After a year in prison, during which I had longed for the outside world, when the day came for our release, I felt unhappy at leaving some of the young convicts who had become my friends. There would be no bright-eyed Bachuli who took her life sentence as a matter of course, who had chatted gaily to me of her happy life before she was married and who hummed mountain ditties all the time she was working. There would be no Alaka to go back to and visit as we had so often planned, as she was dead. There were numerous others who had become dear to me and whom I was loath to leave.

The day of my departure dawned and I went round bidding farewell to my fellow politicals as well as to the convicts and a few wardresses who had learnt to shed their hard exterior and had behaved quite humanely towards us. Suddenly two arms were flung round me and turning I saw my beloved Bachuli, her large grey eyes filled with tears, standing unable to utter any word. I embraced her and turning her face towards me said, 'You must always be brave, Bachuli, and try to be as happy as is possible here. When you are released, let me know and if you want to come to me you will always have a home.'

'You will not forget me in the great big world outside,' she sobbed. 'They tell me here that no one likes to remember a convict friend once they are outside.' I stroked her short matted hair and assured her that it would not be so. For nearly two years I kept in touch with Bachuli through whoever amongst my friends was sent to Lucknow Gaol. Then I heard she was transferred and though I tried hard I lost track of her, but I hoped she would turn up one day. She never did, and though a great many years have passed her memory is as fresh with me as it was before and I think it will always remain so.

As I left the gaol I turned to have one last look at the grim and forbidding walls of my prison home. The large iron gates were slowly closing and through them I could see the young convicts who had just bid me farewell. My heart was heavy but I tried to smile and waved to them. Then I turned away quickly to wipe the tears I could not control. The women politicals who were released with me laughingly asked me whether it was breaking my heart to leave gaol. They little understood for whom my tears were shed, for they had never cared to know the convicts as I had done. Nor were they disturbed with the visions that I had of these girls spending long dreary years behind those walls—simple innocent creatures condemned by circumstances over which they had no control to an existence within high walls, away from a normal family life and those who loved them. It was for these young girls who through sheer misunderstanding and cruelty were forced to commit crimes that ordinarily they would never have committed, that my heart bled. Poverty, neglect and custom had combined to make them what they were—and though longing to get back home I felt sad at having to leave them. I was returning to my home, to the warmth and love of family and friends—all waiting to welcome me while they—what of them and their future, I wondered? But I dared not think.

WARRANT TO NOWHERE

By *Walter Musgrave*

IT was noon on a bitter day in mid-January. Sleet whipping in from the Irish Sea stung our faces and ears, and slid in icy droplets down our necks. One of the governor's rules was that prisoners were not allowed to turn the collars of their raincoats up.

Most of us worked indoors in the winter months. Some sewed buttons on shirts, some darned socks, others packed vests and pants into laundry baskets for Borstals and closed prisons in various parts of the West country, and still others ripped open copper cables and extracted the wire for sale to the scrap merchants.

The sheds and outbuildings where these occupations were carried on, were heated by coke stoves, and lighting and stoking the stove provided two men from each party with time-killing work. Wood and coke had to be fetched from the store. While one man split the wood with a hand-axe another took a sledge-hammer and broke up huge resin-impregnated discs that sent flames roaring up the chimney the moment they caught alight.

Indoors or out, summer and winter, we wore heavy black boots and gaiters. It was the rule, for the governor who had been in some yeomanry regiment, liked to show his authority by playing at soldiers.

This was an Open Prison, within smell of the sea, yet in sight of nothing but mud flats and tussocks of grass flattened by the wind. And between the prison and Greenland there was no windbreak save that offered by Ireland.

In each dormitory an orange covered book hung on a peg by the door. This was the book of regulations issued in London. But the 'official' regulations were supplemented by a variety of local rules made by the governor who exercised his 'discretion' to the full. He preferred to transmit his decrees by word of mouth from Chief to Principal Officers, from warder to warder, from warder to prisoner, and in the event of confusion to advise the prisoner. 'Obey the last command you received.'

The system had advantages. Prisoners were kept in a constant state of suspense, not knowing whether the latest *ad hoc* rule was a whim of the governor, the invention of a warder, or an edict from the Prison Commissioners. And the governor could, and often did, extract himself from the confusion of conflicting rules by the simple expedient of saying innocently, 'I gave no such instructions,' or 'I must speak to Mr. Thrasher. He could not have understood what I said.'

A little Siberia it was, visited by geese but not by 'prison visitors'. The 'inmates' were Scots, Welsh, Irish, English, mostly from midland and west-country prisons, some from London, a few from the North. Jamaicans, Turks, Cypriots, Indians, and Chinese added the spice for variety. But none were supposed to be in for violence and most had never been in prison before. For five years there had been no case of assault, and few men had risked being caught by the treacherous Atlantic tides in an attempt to escape. The place had no need for walls or wire or even for the galaxy of grim-faced warders in blue who seemed so busy but did so little.

*　　　　*　　　　*

On this particular day three hundred and fifty of us were on parade. We were drawn up by working parties, each party of thirty or forty prisoners in three ranks under the eye of two or more warders. Five parades were held daily in addition to check counts at meals, in the work sheds, and in the dormitories when the doors were locked at night and unlocked at six in the morning.

Objecting to the mixture of kindergarten and recruit-training methods new arrivals often applied to be returned to a closed prison where warders left prisoners in peace and petty discipline was less irksome. Such requests were received with contempt.

In charge of each parade was a Principal Officer. As each warder in charge of a party bawled out the number of prisoners in the ranks the Principal Officer would check the figure against that listed by the Main Office. Recounts were frequent.

Jeers and cat-calls rose from the ranks. Men hungry for dinner or tea would shout out : 'Can't you count you silly f———?' 'Hold your f———tongues,' came back the chorus from the men in uniform. After nine months in this long tunnel of fear and misery I had grown philosophical. It was unbelievable that the pin-prick of light was about to burst into day.

'Fall out tomorrow's and Monday's discharges,' shouted Kitson, the Principal Officer in charge. He had a cherubic smile but the cunning of a hyena. For months, weeks, days, hours I had been praying for this call to freedom. But now I felt para-lysed as though the sleet and the wind were mocking me, as though the command was another of those terrifying dreams which had so often brought me crashing against my locker in the dark of the night. 'Come on, come on,' shrieked Kitson from the shelter of the wash-house porch. 'Go on, Walter,' urged my neighbour, 'it's all over man. Hurry, for God's sake.'

I marched quickly to the white line by the wash-house and turned about facing the parade. But even now I could not be-lieve that beyond the mud-flats and the monstrous estuary was a world of men, women, and children, a world of peace and laughter, a world of fresh milk and eggs and meat and butter and fruit. Only the icy blast from Greenland or the Arctic jerked me into the knowledge that this was indeed the end of the tunnel.

Beside me stood a long, haggard man I scarcely knew, but who had offered me a lift to London in his brother's Jaguar. His name was Henfield. For many years he had worked as an accountant in Costa Rica. His wife and two children had been drowned in a hurricane. Henfield had returned to England and taken to drink. He had served ten months for reckless driving while drunk; here was a man who needed compassion and treatment, not imprisonment.

To the left of us stood twenty-five other prisoners, but we were the only two due to be discharged. The others were to seek the governor's permission to write special letters, or to send away a few shillings of their money as presents to their wives and children. Some were applying for Petition Forms, imagining that somebody would take pity on them and move them to a gaol nearer their homes or do something to prevent their families falling to pieces.

Kitson motioned us to move off, and as we trudged up to the Star Chamber I thought of the three petitions I had submitted and the immense trouble I had gone to in cutting down the words to a minimum. I thought too of the forty-six other petitions I had helped my fellow inmates to write . . . and of the futility of it, for not one had succeeded in its purpose. It was, I knew, a typical example of hypocrisy, a trick to induce the prisoner to believe that even inside he was not without hope of relief and help. But what did it matter? Were we not lucky still to be alive?

Some yards behind the straggling, shivering file rolled One-Eyed-Jack, the warder with the weeping eye and dripping nose. He leaned against the wind and the sleet, his collar turned up and his neck protected by a dark blue scarf.

When he had caught up with us he said breathlessly:

'You, Mousegrieve, and you 'Enfield . . . to the 'ead of the file . . . discharges first . . . do up yer f . . . buttons.' One-Eyed-Jack paused to wipe his weeping eye and blow his

nose. Then, giving us a chameleon-like glare, he continued:
'When the Chief rings the bell mount the steps one by one, knock
on the door, give the guv'ner yer name and number ... not
that 'e doesn't know yer by this time ... stand to attention, and
keep yer dirty 'ands orf of 'is table.' Another pause for breath,
a wipe, and a blow. 'And when the guv'nor asks, as 'e 'as to
accordin' to the regulations, "Any complaints?" ... and I don't
doubt you 'ave plenty as I 'ave ... you will say, "No sir" ... unless, of course, yer want another couple of weeks in the cells ...
I'm speakin' for your benefit, Mousegrieve, becorze I know you
'ate 'im as 'e 'ates you ... so if you expect to leave this 'ole to-
morrer you'll keep yer tongue still, otherwise you'll be in here
for two weeks or more while your groundless complaints and
frivl'us charges is bein' hinvestigated.'

One-eyed Jack pottered down to the other end of the line
but finding himself out of the lee of the wooden office, hurried
back.

The bell rang. I climbed the stairs and entered the ante-room
followed by Henfield. The door of the governor's room opened.
On his right stood the Chief Officer, the lean pink man, of whom
prisoners said he had been trained at Belsen. To the left of the
Governor stood the Second Chief Officer, a benevolent moron
with white hair and a tragic expression.

In front of Number Two sat the lean, cadaverous Deputy
Governor. He regarded any prisoner who spoke 'posh' English
as a menace to the classless society. At the end of the table was
the stout rubicund Welfare Officer who did his best to cope
with the many needs of over 400 prisoners, but who had less
authority than the youngest and most inexperienced warder.

The Governor gave me a fishy glance, as though he was a
pike about to devour a small trout. He wore a blue tweed suit
and a tight-fitting green cloth cap.

The charade began.

I gave my name and number.

'Any complaints?'

'None, Mr. Governor.'

'You and I have not seen eye to eye on all occasions, Musgrave,' he said. Was this remorse, I wondered. But I refused to be drawn. I smiled, with disdain perhaps.

He did not pursue the subject.

'Rail Warrant?' he enquired.

'To Perth please, Mr. Governor.' I made up my mind to get away from Branton, away from London, no matter what the Welfare Officer had or had not arranged for me in the way of accommodation.

'Where was this ... this ... this ... where was Musgrave arrested?' the Governor bubbled at the Chief Officer.

'Branton-on-Sea, Sir.'

He swivelled back towards me.

'You'll get a warrant to the place where you were arrested,' he stormed, 'and get out before I make your guts into garters.'

I got out, but as I hurried across the concrete parade ground to the dining hall I knew that anything could happen in the next eighteen hours.

*   *   *

In the dining hall we sat eighteen or twenty to a table, the senior man occupying the place nearest the aisle and the stove. I had occupied this position for some months. For dinner that day there was 'stew'. I couldn't face it. I shovelled my helping into my neighbour's dish. 'Did you poke him in the face?' he asked excitedly. That was the signal for me to give a verbatim account of what had passed between me and the governor. Besides those at my own table a dozen others gathered in the aisle to listen and comment. 'What a bloody liberty.' 'Write to the Home Secretary, Walter.' And quite unprintable comments.

At the back of the mob in the aisle stood the long, gaunt figure of Henfield. He leaned over and spoke in a loud whisper.

'Every word Walter has told you is true. I heard it. It's just too bad we can't get a tape-recording to send the Archbishop of Canturbury.' But why the Archbishop should be in the least interested in the affairs of a bunch of atheists inhabiting the place that God reputedly by-passed I never understood. It was not that we were atheists by nature or by conviction, but by the will of the Avenging Giant who incited such bestialities and sadism under the cloak of progress and enlightenment.

From the parade at a quarter to two Henfield and I were again called out. This time it was to go through the same rig-marole with the doctor. Stripped to the waist in the cold passage I came to the conclusion that the only hope of surviving the next fifteen hours was to laugh at the Prison Commissioners, the Establishment, the Governor, and most of all at myself.

'Musgrave,' bellowed the doctor's screw.

First I was weighed. I had dropped 17 lbs. in ten months. Not bad, I thought, to weigh 5 lbs. less at the age of 60 that at 24. I regretted the change of emphasis.

'Very satisfactory,' commented Halkett the screw. 'Musgrave has put on 3 lbs. since he came from Wormwood Scrubs.'

The doctor noted it down. He was a little grey-haired man from Lancashire and he had an irritating way of gazing at you as though ruminating. But nothing profound emerged.

He gave me a bovine stare as though he had forgotten the next motion laid down by the rules. The screw coughed, and began tapping his left foot on the worn linoleum.

'Any complaints?' asked the doctor.

'None,' I replied.

'Feeling all right?'

'Fine, thank you.'

'And is your arm recovered from that unfortunate spill?'

'It works, more or less,' I said.

Once again he stared ahead in deep contemplation.

'I believe you have had rather a rough time here, Musgrave. I hope you will find smoother water outside. Put your vest and shirt on.'

The screw busied himself washing out medicine glasses and throwing bits of blood-stained gauze and cotton wool into the bin.

'I hope you won't bear us any ill-will, Musgrave,' the doctor rambled on. 'We have to keep to the straight and narrow path, you know. It is very galling for those who have had a good education and are accustomed to seeking ways and means of saving time and money.'

'It's been an instructive experience,' I said coldly, 'but not one I want to repeat.'

'Well, goodbye and good luck.' We shook hands. The screw looked horrified and angry.

I waited for Henfield in the passage. What a miserable job for a man with a scientific training, I thought. For the doctor knew quite well that it was the fight with two young warders, when I had refused to stand up and call them 'Sir' in the dormitory, that had caused the torn ligament in my arm. The same kind of 'accident' accounted for young Hobson's three cracked ribs, officially described as 'the result of a collision while playing football.' In fact it was caused by numerous jabs of Fenner's truncheon in the damp silence of 'the chokey'. Fenner spent most of his time down at 'the Gate'. He was sallow-faced, and his steely eyes spelt out cold, calculated cruelty.

*   *   *

At supper . . . 'cocoa' made with water which I never touched . . . I thought my hopes of getting away the next morning were finished, for as I was leaving the dining hall a dozen men, then twenty, and very quickly a hundred, rose from their chairs and shouted out, 'Good old Walter . . . the best of luck'. I shouted out my thanks and waved to them. Then, my heart fairly pounding with anxiety, I hurried across the parade ground to my hut.

As the men drifted into the hut after 'supper' they told me that a dozen warders had charged up and down the aisle yelling

'Shut up, sit down you bastards,' and into the fray had bundled Kitson, bereft of his cherubic smile, threatening arrest for mutiny, writing down half a dozen names in his note book, and boasting that you, you and you, 'will go back to Wandsworth.'

*   *   *

I thanked God when I heard the night-watchman clattering up the steps of the hut and saw his torch flashing from bed to bed on his way to call me. For fear of arrest I had not slept, and at 5.30 I was already dressed and had rolled up my bedding for transfer to the Reception office for the final check.

I went to each man who had been woken by the thumping tread of the night-watchman and bade him goodbye. Then I gathered up my bundles and left, praying that never again would I see heavy black boots, gaiters, and chipped enamel mugs, or hear men, half-crazed, shout, cry and giggle in their dreams.

Two hours passed. Our blankets and prison clothes were found correct, and we signed for the return of our civilian clothes and personal possessions.

The screw in charge of Reception handed me an envelope from the Welfare Officer. It contained notes to the National Assistance Board, to the Secretary of a charitable organization at Branton, to the Employment Exchange, and to the Ministry of Pensions. At the last moment, just as the Meat Wagon drew up to take us down to the station, the Chief Officer sauntered in and gave me a pound note with the compliments of the D.P.A., 'as it is Saturday and you may not find the National Assistance Board open on Saturday afternoon.'

At the Gate we jumped off the Meat Wagon and ran across to the grey Jaguar. We stopped for breakfast at the Green Dragon.

Never could I have believed that porridge with fresh un-skimmed milk could taste so good, or that poached eggs on buttered toast would be so appetising, or what a relief good coffee would be after months of watery low grade tea. . . .

The Henfields put me down at Waterloo. For several minutes I stood watching the crowds, the bookstalls, the tobacco kiosks, the fruit stalls, and the barrows of luggage labelled Cunard, Union Castle, Ellerman. I felt as though I had opened my own coffin and had walked out to find the world not much changed. But I was alone, friendless. I wanted to talk with somebody. It didn't matter who. I did not have long to wait, for just behind me I heard a child sobbing. A little boy of four or five was sitting on a large green canvas-covered trunk. He was rubbing his hands together in desperation.

'My Mummy's gone,' he said reproachfully.

'I'll stay with you till she comes back,' I said, and held his hand. He stopped sobbing. He just heaved now and again. I hurried to the fruit stall and bought a box of dates.

'My name's Robin,' he said, cheering up. 'They're nice, but they're rather funny,' he said after eating five or six dates.

I told him that during the war I used to have a bunch of dates hanging outside my tent and I used to eat hundreds.

'You've been nice to me,' said Robin, 'like my Daddy was. If my Mummy doesn't come back will you take me with you?'

'Your Mummy will come back,' I insisted. But I wondered what kind of domestic tangle I had let myself in for so unwittingly. Soon I was conscious of a cloying perfume, and saw a short blousey woman, heavily made-up. As I rose from the trunk she smiled stupidly over the edge of a mousy fur collar.

'How naishe of you to comfort my shild (hic), while I went and had a sh . . . short drink. I shinsheerly trusht he hash behaved hisshelf.'

Poor little Robin! I gave him sixpence for some sweets and then walked to the Ticket Office to change my Warrant. The clerk turned it over, noting the words 'Prison Commissioners'.

'This is no good to me,' he said sourly, 'you should have changed this at Hasselford.'

'I came by car to London, and saved British Railways the trouble of transporting me nearly two hundred miles,' I protested. But he was unmoved. Two hours later I reached Branton Station, surged through the barrier with the crowd of week-enders, and shoved my warrant into the hand of the ticket collector. I crossed the street for the bus to take me into town, but was quite prepared to find that Mr. F. K. Gerrard, the Organizing Secretary of the charity, named on my note of introduction, was not at home to callers on Saturdays. But I was wrong, and the three Victorian villas, which served as offices and interviewing rooms, were a hive of activity.

*   *   *

In the Waiting Room on the first floor two elderly women and a young man carrying an infant were sitting on a bench browsing through ancient issues of *Country Life* and the *Illustrated London News*. On the inside of the door hung a large ornate calendar headed with the name of the organization, its Patron, its President, Vice Presidents, Chairman, Council Members, and in bold italic letters 'Organizing Secretary: Francis K. Gerrard, Esq.' This imposing list included two peers, one Q.C., a Dame, a pair of knights, and several councillors and local potentates I knew by name. I began speculating which of these would be the best bet for a job.

The Q.C. was, I remembered a director of several large public companies, but my first problem was to get hold of a typewriter and copy out several dozen 'Records of Career' complete with references.

My plans were cut short by the sudden entry of a miniature Diana Dors who said sharply : 'Ken A help you?' I said I had a personal note to Mr. Gerrard and handed it to her.

'This way, if you please.' I followed a taut swaying posterior supported on stiletto heels through a maze of chairs and tables to a glass box-like room in the far corner.

'Thair is Mr. Gerrard's office,' she pointed majestically. 'Haire is your note. Kaindly knock before entering,' and she strutted away to a desk by the window. As the door was wide open and the occupant was already on his feet there seemed no point in knocking. He was a bony ginger-haired man with bright blue eyes and a sharp inquisitive nose.

'Mr. Musgrave . . . from Hasselford Prison . . . delighted to meet you, my dear chap.' He spoke loudly so that the whole office must have heard. We shook hands with vigorous insincerity. 'I was looking out for you yesterday,' he continued. He did not ask me to sit down. He showed no inclination to shut the door.

I said I had come as quickly as I could and that I had only been released at 8 o'clock that morning.

'Ah well,' he soliloquised, 'when correspondence passes through several hands errors are bound to creep in, are they not?' I managed to edge my way past a large steel filing cabinet so that what I said would not inevitably be overheard by the staff in the General Office. I thought it best to come to the point at once.

'My first two priorities are accommodation and work, Mr. Gerrard. I daresay the Welfare Officer has given you some idea of my background. Next I must get my luggage out of store and somehow I should like to get the loan of a portable typewriter.'

He smiled sardonically. Then he took a cigarette from a leather case and lit it with a gas lighter. Ostentatiously I took the last of my Woodbines from its paper packet and asked him for a light.

'I have done what I can, my dear fellow. But you confront me with great difficulties, I assure you. However I am glad to say my friend Mrs. Tonkin, 71, Old Mill Lane, has agreed to put you up . . . and on Monday you will of course report to the National Assistance Board, the Employment Exchange, and the Pensions Office. They will show you every sympathy and consideration, I am sure.' Evidently I was not going to get any help over my luggage. 'I hope Mrs. Tonkin will not expect me to pay in advance, Mr. Gerrard, as I can't, and won't she think it a bit odd of me to turn up without any luggage?'

Mr. Gerrard pursed his lips, and then with that sardonic smile he said : 'Cross your bridges when you come to them, my dear chap. You are a free man now. You have paid your debt to society,' and then rubbing his hands with satisfaction at a task well done he added, 'If I can be of any further help to you, please don't hesitate to let me know.' And with that he led me through the General Office to the head of the stairs.

In spite of the breakfast at the Green Dragon and the box of dates shared with Robin I was hungry. I had 38/- left of my own money and the pound from D.P.A. As I walked down the main street towards the sea I was conscious of a strong smell of grilling meat. It was the Mermaid, the best known Grill Room in the town. 'Rump Steak, Porterhouse Steak, Fillet Steak, Chump Chops, Spring Chicken (half), Braised Celery. . . .' I wrenched myself away from that costly menu and a few doors further on I bought a carton of milk and three sponge cakes. Across the road was a derelict bomb site, whose jagged walls were overgrown with ivy. Protected from the east wind I sat down and ate my lunch as though I was a tourist enjoying his first trip to Sorrento. There was something so unnatural about the silence that I kept listening for the prison siren, the dining hall bell, and the shouting of the screws and the prisoners. But the peace was short-lived.

From behind the wall appeared a policeman. I went on drinking from my carton.

'This is private property,' he announced sternly, 'if you want to eat in the open there's the beach or the promenade.'

He wandered off, wrote down the particulars of two cars parked by the curb, and disappeared. For three or four minutes I sat in the sun, although there was no real warmth in it.

The Tonkin house was one of a long row of mid-Victorian dwellings each with identical bow-windows and stone steps, all

11

of three floors and roofed with slates. It was a narrow drab lane but within a few minutes of the sea.

In one window I read, 'Bed and breakfast. No Coloureds or children,' in another : 'Alterations and mending by expert machinist,' and then, in the bow window of No. 71, 'Bed and breakfast, sorry no dogs or birds.'

The front door was painted pale lilac and beneath the chromium bell-push the order in red plastic letters, 'Press Once and Wait'. I pressed. From behind the door came the sound of Big Ben striking the quarter hour, the pitter-patter of feet on boards or lino, followed by a girl's urgent call, 'Mum, take the pins out of your hair. There's a gent at the door.'

A squat, jovial little woman in emerald velvet opened the door, but she had not taken the pins from her golden curls.

'Are you the gent from Mr. Gerrard?' she enquired gaily, 'Come along in dear, isn't the weather something cruel?'

To forestall her I said my luggage would arrive in a few days.

'That's all right, dear, I've kept the best room in the house for you . . . Number Three on the first floor,' and she led the way up a steep yellow carpeted staircase into a large room with a bow-window, plush orange curtains tied back with chrome-yellow ribbon, a double bed with brass knobs, a marble topped washstand with cerise basin and jug, and a gilt mirror over a gas fire.

As the squat little body hurried round the room flicking dust off the kidney shaped dressing-table and the primrose chest of drawers I thought I had better find out how much this 'best room in the house' was going to cost.

'Well, it's the off-season now dear, so I can do you for Five guineas weekly including one bath. But gas has gone up so any extra baths will be one and six. I do the cooking myself so I'm sure you won't have any complaints, and I provide a mid-day meal on Sundays. My husband always said I was the best cook in the world . . . that is, until he was taken.'

Taken by what, I wondered. By death, by the police, by some

other woman? No matter, Mrs. Tonkin gave me a feeling of warmth, confidence, humanity. She was the very reverse of the typical English seaside landlady, and a strange choice for that mean-eyed Mr. Gerrard to make.

When she came to the small table by the bed she gave a little laugh and pointed to a large picture in a white frame.

'I hope you're not analergical to holy pictures, Mr. Musgrave. Truth is it's supposed to be Our Lord. Never could see the likeness meself, but when I had the kitchen painted I hadn't the heart to throw it out. You know how superstitious women are. I could put it in the toilet if you prefer.'

'It won't bother me in the least,' I assured her.

She gave the glass a good dusting so that the overweight angels and tree-carrying doves would get a better view of the gas fire.

'I expect you'd like a cuppa in the morning, dear. I usually charge sixpence, but we'll say it's included in this case, shall we?'

I thanked her for her kind action. And then a haunting notion came over me. Had Gerrard told her where I had come from? Without my knowing it, had this friendly comfortable Mrs. Malaprop and I got something in common? Well, if she wanted to tell me she would. I was not going to probe. When she closed the door I turned on the gas fire and found that the last occupant had left about two shillings worth unused. She had done far more. In the top drawer of the painted chest I found an unopened packet of Lucky Strikes, a pad of blue writing paper and envelopes, a pale blue lace-edged handkerchief embroidered with the initial 'L', a brand new pair of nylon stockings marked 9/11d, and a picture postcard of the Chateau Frontenac Hotel at Quebec.

I sat down in front of the gas-fire and asked myself what my late moral instructors would have done with these finds. The answer was not long in coming.

The door opened. 'I'm Nancy,' announced a twenty year old edition of Mrs. Tonkin, 'Mum thought you would like some tea and a piece of cake after your journey.' She put the tray on the small table by the bed and brought both to me by the fire. 'How very kind of you both,' I said.

'I'm afraid the room's a bit stuffy, Mr. Musgrave, but it hasn't been occupied since Leonora left for Canada just before Christmas.'

'I don't know anything about Leonora, Nancy, but she left in a hurry?'

'Well, yes . . . she did . . . but how did you know?'

Nancy poured out my tea.

'Because she left some stockings, a handkerchief, some note-paper. . . .'

'Oh, I am sorry, Mr. Musgrave. Please don't say anything to Mum. I was supposed to clean out the drawers. She'd be furious if she knew I'd forgotten.'

I promised to say nothing.

'Leonora ran off with her boy-friend. He's a Canadian with pots of money. Her step-mother tried to stop her, but he fetched her from here about two o'clock one morning and they went straight to the boat at Southampton. They're married now. Well, I've finished with strip-tease too. As soon as Mum sells the house I'm going in for drama.'

'What am I to do with Leonora's bits and pieces, Nancy?'

'Anything . . . anything, Mr. Musgrave, as long as Mum doesn't know.'

*   *   *

My conscience was clear. Short of taking the things out of the drawer and asking her to take them away what could I do? I had better accept Leonora's gift with gratitude.

When I had finished my tea I took the stockings round to Kell and Harrison, the store in Crown Road, and asked to see the manager.

'I don't expect you usually exchange goods,' I said, 'but

would it be possible to take these stockings and let me have a pair of woollen socks instead?'

'Most certainly, sir,' he replied to my astonishment, and I handed him the handkerchief as well as the stockings.

Ten minutes later I was back in my room with a pair of fawn, blue, and red fair isle socks, and 7/3 change. With the aid of Leonora and luck I decided to write five letters, smoke three or four Luckies, and then have a good solid meal. I had a hunch that this kind of fortune could not last.

Over the grilled sole at the Mermaid I tried sorting out the Tonkin riddle. Was she an ex-night club queen, a retired priestess of some call-girl establishment or the discarded 'doll' of an upstart plutocrat, and what was the meaning of 'before he was taken'? Two things were clear. She had a heart of gold. She had suffered some tragedy. But why was she running a small boarding-house in Branton? And as I tried fitting the pieces together the sight of Robin and his gin-drinking mother kept floating across the table. Why had she got drunk? What had become of Robin's 'daddy'? What would happen to Robin?

Later that night I cursed myself for a fool. In my predicament it was sheer extravagance to waste thought on other people's problems, knowing that I was powerless to do anything. Self-preservation dictated that I should adopt the armadillo-like protection acquired by Mr. Gerrard.

At a quarter to ten on Monday morning I called at the National Assistance Board office in Hertford Street. A short thick-set man with white hair and drooping moustache opened the note I had brought from the D.P.A. He looked at me over the top of his bi-focals as much as to say, 'Ah, an outcast,' and invited me to a seat in the third of seven cubicles.

Then he began the inquisition. My full name, year and date of birth, place of birth, marital state, occupation, last address, present address; had I reported to the Employment Exchange and why not; did I possess any government bonds, stocks, shares, property, or Post Office savings; was anything due to me from the Ministry of Pensions and National Insurance and why not; where was my insurance card; were any debts due to me; had I any dependents; were they drawing benefits; had I ever applied for National Assistance before and where . . . All this he wrote down, filling four pages and half-filling the fifth. Then he said, 'What rent are you paying?'

'Five guineas weekly, including one bath and a mid-day meal on Sundays, bed and breakfast on other days,' I replied.

'Preposterous,' he exploded. 'I am not surprised . . .' He thought better of it and stopped.

'It was arranged, as you probably know, by Mr. Gerrard who acts for the D.P.A. in this town.'

'If I have taken down your replies correctly, kindly sign here,' he said. I signed. He took the papers and disappeared down the passage, leaving me to absorb the heated altercations in the two neighbouring cubicles from which I was separated by green banana shaped partitions.

Ten minutes passed, and in that time I learnt a lot about Mrs. Martlet and her seven children and the pathetic case of Mr. John Hannibal Grimstone, former civil servant in West Africa.

A younger official now confronted me. He sat down and poured over the papers.

'A somewhat unusual case, Mr. Musgrave. Have you no relatives who would assist you?' I said I had not.

'And you took no action to secure a position before you left er . . . er . er . . Hasselford?'

'I made repeated applications for special letters to send to possible employers, but they were refused.'

'That is not the information given to us, I may say . . . however . . . I must take your word for it.'

'If you are suggesting that I am lying I suggest you try a dose of prison yourself and see how you get on. Do you seriously imagine I would come near this office unless I was driven to it?' His insinuations, his smugness, his impudence made me furious.

'Very well, very well, but it is not necessary to get aerated.

We shall do what we can to assist you. But you will have to be visited, of course. Until then we can make you a grant of £3.10.0.'

'Which does not cover one week's bed and breakfast,' I said acidly.

'Kindly take a seat on one of these benches and when the cashier is ready he will call out your name.'

I had been very slow to realize that my sentence did not begin when I was led in handcuffs from the Court to Wormwood Scrubs, but on my release. I decided that I must see Mr. Gerrard immediately, for what was the meaning of 'After-Care' if responsible officials could do no better than land one in this kind of mess?

I had been sitting on the bench for about five minutes when my name was called out, but the bidding was not from the cashier's window. I hurried down the row of cubicles and there in the last one stood a tall man of obvious importance, for he wore a dark red waistcoat and white carnation in his buttonhole.

'Sit down, Mr. Musgrave. I understand from my colleague that you have taken accommodation at Five Guineas weekly for bed and breakfast. I must make it clear that such an exorbitant charge far exceeds the Board's scale.'

'I did NOT take this accommodation,' I retorted in a tone of exasperation, 'it was arranged for me by Mr. Gerrard who must surely know your regulations.'

'But you should have declined the offer, Mr. Musgrave. You should have declined it the moment you were informed of the heavy expense.'

'How could I on a Saturday?' I demanded, 'do you seriously expect me to sleep on the beach in mid-winter and to risk being picked up for vagrancy?'

'There is no advantage in being ridiculous, Mr. Musgrave. Quite apart from the de luxe area you have chosen we do not care to encourage prepared meals.'

From the next cubicle a falsetto voice called out, 'Go it guv'nor, hit 'em where it 'urts.' The interruption gave me a moment to reflect.

'I don't understand what you mean by prepared meals. Are you proposing that I should exist on raw meat or on frozen dishes? Please explain.'

Now it was his turn to show signs of irritation.

'No, no, no. You should take a room with cooking facilities such as a gas ring or the share of a kitchen and bath, not a place where a landlady makes large profits from the meals she serves.'

'I cannot undo what has been done on my behalf,' I said without any show of 'aeration', 'but I must point out that if Mrs. Tonkin asked me for one week's payment in advance and I could not pay she would be quite entitled to call the police, who, I don't doubt, would have the greatest pleasure in arresting and charging me with fraud. In that case I should have no choice but to call Mr. Gerrard, the Welfare Officer, and you yourself as witnesses.'

'That's the stuff,' came the falsetto voice again.

'Shut up, you,' shouted my third questioner.

'Very well, Mr. Musgrave, we will leave it at that for the moment. The cashier has your £3.10.0 ready now.'

It was a few minutes to twelve when I left the N.A.B. My time schedule had gone awry. I had no clean underclothes, no pyjamas, and no clean shirt. 'To hell with it,' I said to myself and immediately set off for Young and Goodbody, the furniture store which had my two trunks.

'You're in luck, sir,' said the clerk in charge of removals, 'we're delivering some stuff to Old Mill Lane this afternoon, so you can rely on your trunks being at Mrs. Tonkin's by four o'clock. That will be £2 for the storage and we shan't need to charge you for delivery.'

From there I walked up the Mall and realized that I was both tired and hungry. Arguments and rudeness I find far more exhausting than long walks by the sea or hours of typing in a cold and airless room. I kept on thinking of this quaint expression 'prepared meals'. A 'prepared meal' I was going to have and I was going to enjoy it, and take my time. This time it was thick oxtail soup followed by two grilled herrings with soft roes, and I spent nearly an hour over it.

I then felt strong enough to tackle the Employment Exchange nearly a mile away, and to take Mr. Gerrard at his word. At the Exchange were three queues of men lined up in front of counters. Not being queue-minded I went out into the passage, found a stone staircase, and trotted up to the first floor.

As several men emerged through some swing doors I went in and found myself in a large office with some twenty desks each with a card index. Behind each desk sat a man or woman, and the desks were labelled 'clerical workers', 'shop assistants', 'casual labour', and 'building trades'.

A game of musical chairs seemed to be in progress, for the moment an applicant sitting opposite an interviewer got up to leave, a man, from among the dozen or so standing by the door, ran to the vacant chair and occupied it. It was only five minutes before I landed with a crash on the chair in front of the desk marked 'Building Trades'.

'Are you registered?' asked an amiable middle-aged woman.

I said that I was not, and I handed her my tell-tale note from Hasselford. She looked alarmed. I assured her I was harmless. But she would not take my word for it and called in a male clerk, who asked for my yellow card and my insurance card. I handed over the yellow card, but explained that as yet I had no insurance card. 'Have you been paid?' he asked.

I said, 'Yes, but not enough.'

This seemed incomprehensible. Both disappeared and went into a huddle with two other clerks behind a clear glass partition. After much shrugging of shoulders and raising of eyebrows an older man came to the table.

'I understand you are seeking clerical work,' he said, 'and the note you brought states that you have a university degree.'

I said that was quite correct, and furthermore I had acted as Judicial manager of two large businesses abroad and had got them off the rocks, and that I had long practical experience of management accounting. I added hastily that I was handicapped by an injury to my right arm, and I found it better to type everything, even draft letters for typists and office memos.

He gave me a dead-pan look. 'We have nearly five hundred men of forty and upwards, many with excellent references and great experience, seeking even part-time work,' he said lugubriously.

'So you can offer nothing, not even at £12 to £15 a week?'

'A greengrocer at the east of the town is prepared to pay an experienced salesman and driver £8.5.0 weekly,' he said, 'but there's your insurance card. I can see difficulties arising.'

'I feel like a rat in a trap,' I said, 'I cannot get work here and without work I cannot meet my living expenses.'

At this point another official came to the desk. 'Mr. Musgrave, I believe,' he began as though emulating the welcome Stanley gave to Livingstone, 'I think it might be useful if we had a little chat in privacy,' and he motioned me to the section of the office behind the glass partition. There we were joined by the original woman, and three men.

The first said, 'I think it would clear our minds, Mr. Musgrave, if you told us why you were sent to prison. I appreciate that it is a delicate matter but unfortunately it is the kind of thing that follows you like a ghost.'

I gave them a resumé of the whole story.

'A magistrate's court,' exclaimed the first.

'Surely they exceeded their powers,' said the second.

'One hears too many stories of the police similar to this,' observed the fourth.

The woman said, 'It looks to me as Mr. Musgrave ought to have appealed.'

The senior who had held his fire, said : 'A savage sentence for what seems a technical offence. There was obviously no intention to commit fraud. Had you gone to Sessions you would never have been found guilty.'

'It's too late to undo what has been done,' I said, 'I have blotted my escutcheon and anybody who chooses can find it out.'

'The trouble is you lay yourself open to blackmail even if you do land a job,' said the elder man. 'What then? I can't see the police in this town taking much interest in the fate of an ex-prisoner, can you George, or even the Chief Constable for that matter?'

The woman interjected, 'Subject to what my colleagues say I feel that you should go to some industrial centre, London or Birmingham, or where you would be lost in the crowd and employers would not concern themselves with anything but your references, which are excellent, and your personality.'

'And if I took your advice where do I raise the money for the fare and for moving my luggage?' I asked.

'That is not our function,' remarked the elder man firmly, 'but I am confident the National Assistance Board would show you practical sympathy. After all you don't want to remain on their hands for ever.'

I walked back to Mrs. Tonkin's angry, depressed and tired. But my trunks had arrived and I spent more than an hour unpacking my clothes, putting them away in the cupboards and drawers, and arranging my books.

The following morning I found two official letters for me on the breakfast table. The first was from the N.A.B. to say that a visitor would be calling the next day, but regretting no definite time would be given. The second was a request to call at the Pensions Office 'at your earliest convenience.'

As my financial condition was worsening day by day and I had no means of advertising for a job, even in the local paper, I decided to call on Mr. Gerrard and to find out once and for all whether he was really concerned to help or whether his protestations were mere humbug. In any event I thought that if all those imposing names on the Calendar were ready to assist ex-prisoners they might manage to refund the small amount I had to pay to retrieve my clothes from the store as it was obvious that the N.A.B. would refuse.

It was sunny but cold, and I thought the ten minutes sharp walk would clear my head and give me energy to fight through another day of anxiety and frustration. Where was all this freedom, this right to work, this moral rectitude, this innate urge to help the under-dog? These questions kept coursing through my head as I walked quickly towards Mr. Gerrard's office. For the first time in my life I was beginning to understand why foreigners spoke of 'perfidious Albion', why men went on strike, and why, in spite of the futility of violence, men whose dignity was trampled on by the bureaucracy, who were homeless, who knew their children were not getting enough to eat, rebelled against society and committed crimes. 'What,' I asked myself, 'has the Welfare State accomplished? It has resulted in penal taxation, in the creation of a swarm of officials whose primary concern is not the welfare of the community but the avoidance of the smallest deviation from the printed rules that might lead to loss of promotion or pension rights, and worst of all, it has destroyed the moral obligation of one man to help another in distress.'

As I went up the stairs to Mr. Gerrard's office I felt tired and much older than on the day I had been turned loose from prison. But still, somewhere deep down, was that fierce fire of self-preservation that had seen me through so many crises. It was not extinguished. It needed fuel. It needed fanning. Mr. Gerrard provided the necessary draught. He rose from his desk and gave me a hearty slap on the shoulder.

'Ah, my dear Mr. Musgrave . . . delighted to see you . . . and all your troubles are over . . . or nearly . . . and good Mrs. Tonkin is looking after you well . . . I am sure she is.' He pulled up a chair for me.

'Now Mr. Gerrard,' I began, 'I must be frank with you. Neither you not your organization have any legal obligation to me, but I think you have some moral obligation and that you have been entrusted with certain duties by the Welfare Officer.' He looked pained. His thin lips drew taut, but he said nothing.

I continued, 'Are you aware that the National Assistance Board will not meet Mrs. Tonkin's charges and that technically she could have me arrested for fraud? That is what you have done, Mr. Gerrard. You have risked getting me put back inside, unless of course you intend to make up the difference between what the N.A.B. will allow and the total of Mrs. Tonkin's account.'

'I am shocked at your attitude, Mr. Musgrave. . . .'

'I dare say you are,' I interrupted, 'but I have not finished yet. Quite apart from this board and lodging account I should like to know whether you are prepared to help me find suitable work. Your council includes many well-known local citizens. Are they on the list for self-glorification or do they consider it their duty to give practical help to people like me? If they are ready to help then I suggest you give me a note to four or five and I will undertake to be quite candid with them.'

Mr. Gerrard paled. His mouth moved, but beyond a grunt of vexation, he kept silent. I told him about my clothes and what I had had to pay to get them out of store. I suggested that one of his supporters might be generous enough to refund the money or at least to make a loan until I found work. I said I was sure that somebody must surely be able to lend me a portable typewriter for a month, or to afford a couple of pounds for the hire of a machine. I ended by saying : 'It was not my wish to come to Branton at all. I was compelled to. The Employment Exchange can offer me nothing. If none of these people on your Council are prepared to accept me at face value and to believe what I tell them, I must go elsewhere. In that event are you prepared to pay my fare to London or Birmingham or Manchester?'

He was about to reply when the ersatz Diana Dors brought in a tray with a pot of tea, milk, sugar, biscuits, and one cup and saucer.

'In effect, Mr. Musgrave, you are asking for money . . . cash . . . or a substantial loan,' he began pompously. 'We don't believe in hand-outs. Everybody would be coming to us. It is our policy to encourage all members of the public to stand on their own feet. In your case I went out of my way to help. I actually called on Mrs. Tonkin and asked her personally if, in view of the unfortunate circumstances, she would accommodate you.'

'You told her I had just come out of prison?' I snapped.

'You seem to think that imprisonment is a matter of no consequence, Mr. Musgrave. I assure you that it is not the view of the public, or of my council. You must surely appreciate that I cannot do as you ask. I have my own position to consider. Let me assure you that I am not well remunerated and that I too am heavily taxed. Why, I have had my present car for four years. I should like to replace it, Mr. Musgrave, but I have to be prudent.'

I was on the verge of exploding with anger. But I got up and hurried away before I said anything I might regret. Perhaps I had said too much already. Yet I was convinced that Mrs. Tonkin would do nothing to make my life more difficult. If Gerrard was a charlatan, she, that very queer misfit in Branton, was as genuine and Christian-minded as any woman one could meet.

*   *   *

It was about seven the next morning when I woke up with a stiff constricted feeling across my chest. It was as though a heavy iron bar had landed just below my shoulders, crushing my ribs. It hurt to take a deep breath, but it was not a stabbing pain like pleurisy. My throat was sore and I was hoarse, yet I was sure I had no fever and that it was neither pneumonia nor bronchitis.

Mrs. Tonkin brought my breakfast on a tray and a hot-water bottle. I asked her to stay with me a little while, if she was not busy.

'It's the reaction, dear, after what you've been through. But for God's sake, dear, don't do what my husband did.'

I waited for her to go on, not knowing what to say.

'They put him inside for eighteen months, Mr. Musgrave. Honestly, dear, I know he was innocent. But when he came out he was treated like a dog with mange. People we used to call 'friends' shunned us. We had no friends. His health was broken.

And then one night he said he was going for a long walk so that he would sleep better. I never saw Phil again, except in the mortuary. He walked eight miles to Queen's Hall Farm and shot himself on the edge of the lake.'

'How awful,' I said weakly.

'Of course there was an inquest. The verdict was that he killed himself while the balance of his mind was upset. That's the way they salve their consciences. But they never asked, 'What caused the upset to his mind?' Oh no, dear, but as sure as God is in heaven those nagging coppers will get their deserts. That was four years ago. So you see, dear, I know the suffering you are going through.'

An hour passed. Then the doctor arrived. He was a quiet spoken G.P. of about forty. He sounded my chest, thumped, listened to my heart, examined my throat, pressed my stomach, took my temperature, and tested my reflexes.

'Have you ever been in a car crash?' he asked. I said I had not.

'Or an air crash?' he added.

'Yes, two,' I replied, 'but ages ago.'

'Your right arm seems to have been pretty badly twisted, and that must be quite recent, Mr. Musgrave. However that's only a side-issue. I don't like the look of it. I don't want you to be alarmed, but you have all the symptoms of coronary thrombosis. I shall ask Dr. Kentish to come as soon as he can. Meantime stay where you are, and don't raise your arms above your head.'

I heard him talking to Mrs. Tonkin and then telephoning. I

must have fallen asleep, for the next thing I remember was a tall distinguished diplomat of a man standing by my bed. He wore a dark grey suit with a double-breasted waist-coat.

He asked much the same questions, but threw in for good measure, 'You don't drink heavily, Mr. Musgrave?'

'Good heavens, no. Why do you ask?'

'Dr. Mullins mentioned your right arm, but your left ankle appears to be pretty badly sprained too,' he remarked, 'I agree with Dr. Mullins. We shall get the ambulance right away and I shall give you a more thorough examination in hospital.'

Dr. Mullins said: 'I have spoken to Mrs. Tonkin. She and Nancy will pack up your clothes, but there's no hurry about that. Take it quietly and don't carry anything, not even that small case with your night things.'

For two days I was given a variety of tablets and delicious food but otherwise left in peace. The Matron came for a chat. The Almoner visited me and we found a common chord in East Africa as she had spent three years at Nakuru and one at Eldoret. She was one of those women who seem to pierce one's innermost thoughts without asking a single question or appearing to be curious. I was sure she had hit on the right diagnosis, nervous exhaustion, professionally known as 'hypertension'. Events proved she was a mind-reader, yet without a trace of conceit or self-satisfaction. She had the most attractive speaking voice I have ever heard and the most impeccable pronunciation. I hoped she would come back.

By the third day I was already like a child whose hidden fears of the world have given way to confidence and belief in its parents. The nurses were repairing the damage done by the Avenging Giant.

Treatment of my arm and ankle was undoing the violent mischief done by the two prison warders. My throat was no longer sore. I did not believe that my heart was the real trouble. I needed, and I was getting, regular sleep and plenty of it, regular meals, and freedom from fear.

Behind drawn curtains the two doctors took electrocardiographs, blood pressure, and sedimentation tests. I was wheeled out to the X-Ray Department, where pictures were taken of my chest, arms, and head. For some reason I did not then understand I was being given three egg-nogs daily and massive doses of Vitamin B. My neighbours had meat pie or fish for lunch. I was given two lamb chops or a piece of underdone fillet steak with mashed potatoes and sprouts.

The fifth day of my 'Ritz' treatment was eventful. The Almoner visited me again. We talked of Lake Naivasha, of flamingoes, and impala, and that most beautiful of all the buck family, the sable antelope. 'You know it all so well you ought to write about it,' she said. 'But I'm afraid Kenya has gone. Those who settled there get the blame, while those who made conditions impossible get away scot-free.'

Should I tell her I was dependent on the N.A.B., for money? Should I relate the story of my meetings with Mr. Gerrard? I decided against both. She left me two recent issues of the *National Geographic Magazine* and for an hour I read as though I had no worries to face.

At visiting time that evening the staff nurse asked if I could see a Mr. Armitage. I thought this was a trap set by the police. My suspicions were deepened when she said he had brought what looked like a tape-recorder. But she added that he was most polite and asked if I was really well enough to meet a stranger. Somehow that did not match the manners of the C.I.D., at any rate as I had experienced them.

Mr. Armitage could have saved me from trembling if he had handed the nurse his card instead of bringing it as he introduced himself. 'Henry Ulverstone Armitage, Editorial Director, The Echo', read the card. He said he had heard that I held strong views on the political state of East Africa and knew many of the leading personalities including several Africans.

'Several hundred of our readers are retired people who have served in Kenya, Tanganyika, Uganda, and so forth. Would you have any objection to an article appearing under your name, Mr. Musgrave?'

'None whatever,' I said, 'but unfortunately I have no typewriter here.'

'You have no need for a typewriter, sir. If you agree I propose to put a number of questions to you and we will then record them on this machine, with your answers. From the tape I will then prepare the article and bring the galley proofs for your approval.'

Such business-like and polite methods took me back to the days when I wrote stories for two American papers.

'Do you think the British Government should underwrite the land values of European settlers?' 'Would the economy collapse without the white agricultural community?' 'Is full independence possible without a reversion to tribal warfare?' 'To what extent is communism a danger?' 'Has British export trade suffered as a result of over-appeasement of African ambitions?' 'Do you consider Africans capable of managing the railways, harbours, airports, health, and educational services without European supervision?'

Played back the questions and answers sounded really good. I looked forward to reading the galleys, guessed the article would appear in about ten days, and within six weeks I might receive a cheque for two or three guineas. Mr. Armitage thanked me and departed.

Ten minutes later the staff nurse came back. 'Mr. Armitage asked me to give you this with his compliments,' and she handed me a parcel neatly tied up in scarlet ribbon.

It contained a box of fifty 'Three Castles', a carton of marrons glacés, and a double layer box of chocolate peppermint creams. There was also an envelope with my name typed on it, and in handwriting 'With best wishes for your speedy recovery'. In it were twenty-one brand new ten shilling notes.

Once again I felt I was living in a world of fantasy. For the moment I was so astonished I left the whole lot, money and all, sprawled over my bed. But I could not resist a marron glacé for long. The notes I put back into the envelope and pushed under my pillow. The rest I put away in my locker.

Just before eight the nurses came and drew the curtains round my bed. Dr. Kentish came in, and against all rules, sat on my bed. 'I thought you would like to know that we can find no signs of cardiac trouble,' he began, 'but there must have been a reason for that intense pain and sore throat. We considered a virus infection and discarded it. No signs of lung trouble beyond some old scars. Now, Mr. Musgrave I believe you can tell us more than we can tell you, and I think you should.'

'I can't,' I said.

'Why were you suffering from severe protein deficiency?' Why was your sedimentation test abnormal? What was the cause of this tremor in your hands? Of course anyone can suffer from shock, but a man of your calibre does not suffer from malnutrition . . . normally.'

'I must have been very overtired without realizing it, Dr. Kentish. I suppose interviewing and being interviewed does take it out of you more than you know at the time.'

'We haven't finished with you yet, my friend. You know you winced when I pressed a spot high up in your stomach. We're going to find out what that is all about, and I am ready to bet you an even ten bob it's the start of a duodenal ulcer.'

'Does that mean partial gasterectomy?' I asked airing my limited knowledge.

'I shouldn't think so. I hope not. It should respond to treatment and rest. I'm not one of these knife-happy quacks, Mr. Musgrave.'

On the strength of this good news we each ate a couple of marrons glacés.

As he was leaving he said through the gap in the curtains, 'And if we both gave up cigarettes we should probably live longer.'

For the following fortnight I was allowed to walk up and down the ward and passage in my slippers and dressing gown. The existence of 'some degree of ulceration' was proved by a barium meal and a series of X-Rays. But as they had expected this result and I had been kept off fried food there was no change in my diet.

In the passage was a coin-box telephone. I called Mrs. Tonkin. 'Hello, my dear,' came the cheerful reply, 'I've been so worried about you. To tell the truth I didn't know whether it was my place to come and visit you or not.'

'Oh, Mrs. Tonkin,' I pleaded, 'DO come. I would like to see you. Come this evening if you've nothing else on.'

*   *   *

She came, first of all the crowd of visitors, straight to my bed. Golden curls frilled out from under a saucer-like hat in moss-green surmounted by an exotic mass of Martian-sized violets and lilies of the valley fed all through their plastic lives on the richest hormones. What did it matter that other visitors stared? Little did they know the humility, the kindness, the good humour, and the courage that lay beneath that bizarre baroque exterior.

I said that, before we discussed anything at all I wanted to square my account.

'You don't have to, dear. It's paid!'

'Good heavens, who by?'

'Well, I knew your position. After all that little man from the National Assistance Board didn't call for nothing, did he? So I got on to Mr. Gerrard and I told him it was his responsibility. He booked the room. You were sick and I wasn't going to ask you to pay. Of course, dear, he was put out, but as I said I would be content with $3\frac{1}{2}$ guineas, he jumped at it and sent the cash round by hand. But what will you do when you leave here? I've sold the house, so Nancy and I are going to London. They've given me back my old job at the Ninety Nine. Isn't it wonderful?'

I said I would find some other place in Branton, but if things turned out badly I would come to London.

'And you'll promise to pop in at the Ninety Nine . . . it's in the phone book . . . any time after twelve and we'll have a whisky and a sandwich. I mean it, dear. I hate to think of you being alone here.'

She said some harsh things about Branton in general and Mr. Gerrard in particular, adding that the local government officials were corrupt and the councillors no better than robber-barons. But I was still no nearer discovering what had brought her to Branton. Did it matter? I had a friend, an anchor. Even if her English was that of Mrs. Malaprop and her dress that of an ageing tart she was sincere, sensible, and well able to size up her fellow beings.

She trotted away leaving me two paper-back Maigrets.

I left hospital with a list of things I was to eat and to avoid. And I made a point of calling on the Almoner on my way out. I thanked her for putting Armitage in touch with me. 'I did it for his sake as much as yours, Mr. Musgrave. People tire of parochial news, and as his parents are such charming and generous people I thought I could do everybody a good turn.'

After nine abortive calls at boarding houses I found a small back room at 19 Lammerton Road run by a Mrs. Marchant. She was a lanky, humourless woman of about 50, and she wore thick hornrimmed glasses and a coarse hairnet over sparse mousey hair smarmed down with oil. The weekly charge would be 3 guineas with a simple breakfast plus 10% service, 1/- extra for full breakfast, 1/9 per bath, and 6d. per telephone call, to be written in the book. 'And I don't take guests out of season for less that four weeks,' she announced. It was a decision she was soon to retract.

I phoned for my luggage, which Mrs. Tonkin had had re-collected, and then walked round to the N.A.B. A different clerk attended to me. He went through the same motions and then asked if I was fit to report for manual labour at the Exchange.

Armed with a Doctor's Certificate and my special diet sheet I showed him both documents. He was a long crocodile of a man with a pouchy chin and claw-like hands.

'As you have been in hospital I assume that your circumstances have not changed.' I signed the sheet to that effect, for what had the N.A.B. done while I was in hospital? They had not paid for one newspaper even, and I could scarcely regard the Ten guineas as earnings. It was a gift from heaven and certainly no concern of the crocodile. 'It has been decided to make you a weekly allowance of £4.12.0 which will rise to £4.13.0 in two weeks time,' he said glumly.

'Do I get paid here?' I asked.

'In view of your state of health we shall post you a book of vouchers cashable on Fridays at the London Road Post office,' he droned, 'the cashier will make you an immediate payment of that amount and I should advise you to find cheaper accommodation nearer the railway. Rather different from sunny Africa, I expect, Mr. Musgrave. No lakes, no mountains, no wild life, and everyone you meet a chiseller.'

As he seemed to have time on his hands I asked for his advice about work. At this he threw back his head and chuckled, so that his Adam's apple and pouchy chin bounced up and down in unison.

'Over fifty, my dear sir. Nobody wants men of your age . . . except in Parliament . . . look at me. Do you think I enjoy being hedged in, unable to use my common-sense, crippled by rules, and paid a pittance. My advice is for you to come to terms with yourself. Unless you have influential friends you won't get work and without capital you can't start on your own. Have you got much to live for? I am prepared for death. I have faced the inevitable and laid in my stocks. I can go any time. I can't see a man of your type sharing a room in some gas-chamber like Brixton or putting up with a hostel for long. And there's another thing, my friend . . . don't forget you have got a record, which you will never be allowed to forget . . . never. Your qualifications, your experience, your professional appointments, mean nothing. The cops and the court stripped you of the lot.'

There was something so utterly irreconcilable between National Assistance and these sinister suggestions that the puck in me rebelled. I drew the £4.12.0 and departed, determined that whatever else happened I would not be driven to living in Brixton.

Two days later I had a visit from an N.A.B. visitor. This time there were other questions. Had I any insurance policies? Was I a contributor to the Hospital Savings Fund? On this occasion only one hour was taken up. I signed. He left, slamming the front door. During the afternoon I took two suits to the cleaners, a pile of washing to the laundry, and deposited £5 in the Post Office with the resolve that come hell and high water nothing would disturb that small reserve.

Soon after six that evening Mrs. Marchant stamped into my room.

'Your weekly account, Mr. Musgrave, is payable in advance. And I have changed my mind about the four weeks. Your room is let from the end of your week.'

'That puts me to great inconvenience and needless expense,' I said. 'May I ask the reason for your change of mind?'

'You may. But I don't have to give you any. This is my house . . . a respectable law-abiding house, Mr. Musgrave, and I am not prepared to put up with the kind of man who visited you this morning setting foot on my doorstep, Mr. Musgrave . . . and that's what the position is. You had better try one of those places up by the engine sheds or leave Branton altogether.'

After that scene I went out and had a double whisky at the White Hart, and ate three ham sandwiches. That night I decided I must hire a typewriter and send off at least fifty Records of Career with covering letters, and they must be well-typed. I now had no choice but to give my address as 'Poste Restante, Branton' as I had 'no fixed abode'.

During the following five weeks three other landladies housed and fed me in part until each in turn made some excuse following a visit. Tired of this chasing from pillar to post existence I called on my crocodile man and told him of my experiences. 'Some of these women are very narrow-minded.' That was all he said. I asked if a visit was really necessary every time one moved. 'I didn't make the rules, Mr. Musgrave. But you mustn't forget it's the policy of the State to maintain full employment.' I asked him if he had read Parkinson's Law. He said he had, and he added : 'You should know enough about these things to realize that it's the moral duty of every government employee to make two grow where one grew before.'

'In that case,' I shot back, 'why don't you do your duty and fit me in here ?' He just chuckled.

I kept a list of the letters I sent out and the cost of postage. With each application I enclosed a stamped addressed envelope for the reply. In twelve days the stamp bill came to 61/-. My mailing list yielded nothing. And then, towards the end of the second week, I had a letter from the Pensions Office saying as I had not seen fit to visit them a man from their office would visit me. They gave the date and the approximate time.

He arrived with a statement already prepared. It was to the effect that I disclaimed all rights to benefits. I signed. 'But I never suggested I had any claim,' I said.

'But we have to record it in writing, Mr. Musgrave,' he protested. He then wanted to know why my card was not stamped. This time I let fly. I told him that in prison my maximum wage was 4/6d. weekly payable in kind. Those who smoked paid the government the equivalent of 440% purchase tax. Was anything done to help us on release ? It was not. Did the Probation Officer concern himself with people like me ? No. If the government wanted the cards stamped why did it not authorize the Prison Commissioners to do so ? It was too mean. Even if I got a job and stamped my card would I ever get an old age pension ? The answer was 'no', because I had spent much of my life abroad.

A fortnight later I received a pontifical letter from the Ministry. It said that although I had failed to stamp my card in accordance with the law they had, under the circumstances, decided not to prosecute me. On the spur of the moment I burned with a desire to reply, but what profit is there in kicking concrete?

*   *   *

Towards the end of June I took a long walk inland and came to a new part of the town with modern blocks of flats and well designed shops. I was again looking for accommodation, so I stopped at a stationer's where a large wooden frame enclosed a number of handwritten and typed advertisements. 'Retired Opera Singer gives private lessons.' 'Pedigree Rough Haired Fox Terrier Puppies' . . . 'Almost new Pram' . . . 'De Luxe Private Hotel (Only Europeans)' . . . 'Bed and breakfast (share) 8/6d. per night' . . . 'Lady offers sunny well-furnished room in flat, use of kitchen and bath, breakfast supplied if required. Apply Harriman, 15 Lucerne Court.'

Lucerne Court was a four-storey block, built, I guessed, just before the Second War. There was no lift, but No. 15 was on the first floor.

I rang. 'Wait a minute John,' said a female voice. 'I'm just drying my hands.'

She was tall, grey-haired, with a fresh complexion and blue eyes. 'I'm sorry,' she said, 'I thought it was my son-in-law.'

The room was small, but spotlessly clean, and with a bit of re-arrangement I could see how my things would fit in. I took it, promising to stay at any rate six weeks and paid £2 on account of $2\frac{1}{2}$ guineas weekly rent. As there were no extras and I would now spend time doing my own cooking and washing-up I felt sure the Board would raise my allowance.

Mrs. Harriman told me she was a widow and suffered from asthma, so I must forgive her wheeziness and cough.

I took a bus into the town, packed up my things, and brought them back by taxi.

At eight the next morning Mrs. Harriman brought me a cup of tea and said she had ordered me one pint of milk daily. Details about the laundry, cleaners, and telephone followed. Suddenly she began to cough with such violence I wondered how any heart could stand the strain. Still out of breath she said : 'As a matter of fact I haven't been well enough to work lately, so I'm having to draw the dole, but I want to go away for two weeks in September and by letting this room I shall have the extra few pounds I shall need.'

I said nothing about my own precarious position, but I could see complications looming up.

Later, while I was making some coffee for breakfast, she came into the kitchen. She was still wearing her blue dressing gown. 'Have you anything to do in the town this morning?' she asked.

'I thought of writing some letters here, but why?'

'Well, Mr. Musgrave, it sounds dreadfully rude, but I was wondering if you could be out for a couple of hours . . . say between 10 and 12 . . . as the N.A.B. visitor is coming and I don't want him to find a stranger staying here. It would lead to an inquisition.'

'I'll keep clear until after half-past two,' I said. She seemed much relieved.

I brought back with me cereals, butter, bread, potatoes, two New Zealand lamb cutlets, smoked haddock, sugar, tea, coffee, cos lettuce, cauliflower, bacon, six eggs, and olive oil.

I advised the N.A.B. of my change of address and sent my book of vouchers to have the name of the Post office changed. It came back within two days and the allowance was now £5.3.0 weekly.

Most days Elise Harriman and I would pool our resources, share the cooking and washing-up, and eat in her large bed-sitter which had a balcony. Other than the gnawing anxiety of finding a job my only worry was another visit from the N.A.B.

But they seemed to have lost interest. Perhaps they thought that having brought us together for the world to think what it chose, it would be more tactful to leave us in peace.

Elise knew that I had a continuous struggle to decide my priorities ... eggs, stamps, fruit, stationery ... but not more than that, and I was careful to pay the rent on the day it was due. Sometimes in the evenings we would watch T.V., or drink coffee and play patience. If she went out to friends or to her son-in-law who lived some twenty miles away I would have the run of the flat with Tango, the Burmese cat.

On the 19th of July a furious thunderstorm crashed over the town. The rain smacked viciously against the windows of the sitting room. Then the lights failed, and for half an hour we sat playing patience by candlelight. It was not until nearly midnight that the rage and fury of the storm died down to a distant rumble, and sleep became possible.

Just after five I heard Tango miaowing outside the door. I thought Elise must have gone to the toilet and left her door open. But she was usually so careful not to let the cat out of her room. I turned over and began to doze off again. But again Tango yowled, and from the rise and fall of his cry I thought he must have been shut out and was pacing up and down the passage. I got up to investigate. It was just starting to get light, but there was no window in the passage, and for a moment it did not occur to me why the passage was quite light. Then I realized that Elise's door was wide open, and there stretched across the entrance to her room was her body and her mauve nightdress was drenched in blood. I grabbed her wrist. But there was no pulse beat.

When the doctor came an hour later he said : 'It could have occurred at any time.' There was an inquest and I was called.

*   *   *

I had had enough of Branton. But how could I afford to

pay the fare to London and the charges for moving my things?
If I went to Mr. Gerrard he would make some slighting remark
about what he read in the paper about the inquest and that
would make me very angry. I should get no sympathy from the
N.A.B. There was still the £5 in the Post Office, my gold links,
and my watch. But time was the problem as the agents had
instructions to lock up the flat within 24 hours. Did I dare call
on my benefactor Mr. Armitage, knowing that he had paid me
too much already? Certainly affairs in Africa were coming to
the boil. Without any doubt the obstinacy, muddling, and lack
of realism on the part of the government was sapping the confidence of the many electors who had friends and relations in
East and Central Africa.

He could only say 'No' and my pride could scarcely suffer
from that. I called at the offices of the 'Echo'. Half an hour
later I was on my way to London having paid my fare, the taxi,
tips, and the bill for a meal in the station buffet. The receipt
I signed was for £5 on account of expenses in connection with
a 1,000 word article on government non-policy in East and
Central Africa. I liked Mr. Armitage's 'non-policy' and made
full use of it in my article.

That night I left my luggage at Putney Station and found a
room on the frontiers of Putney and Wandsworth which I
shared with a Negro and a Chinese. But they were both night
workers and did not disturb me until six in the morning. I stayed
in that place three more nights, paying 15/- a night for bed and
breakfast, spending the days hunting for a bed-sitter off the
King's Road or Fulham Road, but fully conscious that I was
being drawn nearer and nearer to Brixton. One woman wanted
three weeks in advance, another a written agreement to stay a
minimum of three months, another demanded four weeks in
advance, a fourth offered an attic room where, being six feet
tall, I would bang my head against the ceiling every time I
went to the chest of drawers or wash basin. After three exhausting
days I found a second floor room with gas fire and ring, fitted

basin, and share of bath at four guineas, which meant a total living cost, without clothes, of about seven pounds. I was just too tired to go on. I took it. The N.A.B. considered my rent to be 'outrageous' and refused to meet it in full, but I showed them my diet sheet and my allowance was raised to £5.9.0d.

I completed the article for the 'Echo' and got a cheque for £5.15.6d. by return, but with a letter. 'Your article is excellent as I was sure it would be. But I am sorry to say we are being merged with the News-Herald which is part of a large group, and they use mostly syndicated material. We accepted the offer because of Death Duties. My father and mother are retiring to Estoril where they have bought a small house, and my wife and I and our two children are leaving for Melbourne in a couple of weeks. I do hope your health is better and that you will soon be on your feet again.'

Another avenue was closed.

I now registered with three private employment agencies in the hope of getting part-time work of some kind. I also became friendly with a fellow lodger of about my own age called John Grierson, who had lost a fortune in Ceylon. He was also trying to find work, and was also on National Assistance. But he had cultivated the Citizens Advice Bureau, who, he said, were most useful at prodding the N.A.B. and persuading them they were dealing with human beings not with cattle to be dipped against tics or inoculated against contagious abortion.

John and I exchanged confidences. He had managed to get a refund of 25/- against his moving cost from Hungerford. His allowance had been stepped up to £5.19.0 as he too was on a special diet because he had diabetes. He told me he had acted as chauffeur to a rich industrialist for five weeks, driving a Rolls, but his employer had died suddenly and the executors wouldn't let him keep his uniform. He had tried the Ministry of Labour at Atlantic House and had had no nibbles in eight months. Advertisements in stationer-tobacconists yielded nothing.

'I have probably become a cynic,' he said pulling at his huge

German pipe, 'but it strikes me as ironical that while the government is forever running into economic crises and exhorting firms to export more, the practical knowledge that men like you and I have, at the receiving end, is just thrown down the drain. Actually,' he said, 'I'm in a bit of a jam. I could probably borrow enough cash to visit Germany and Italy and make arrangements with firms there who would prefer to employ an Englishman who knows the East. But what view would these official myrmidons take? They would say 'If you have friends who are willing to finance your trip to the Continent, they would also help you meet your board and lodging account, so we shall cut you allowance or cancel it. Well, I'm not taking the risk. I've gone through too much to start that argument all over again. So I'm doing the job by correspondence, but I am not optimistic.'

John went over to the gas-ring to brew some coffee.

'What we need is an Ombudsman,' I suggested. John laughed.

'It wouldn't work in this country. You'd need hundreds of them, and each would be surrounded by a flock of clerks appointed to check effective action.'

'Do we have to admit then that the public in this country has grown so docile, so accustomed to being dragooned, so queue-minded that we are no longer a democracy but a lousy mixture of oligarchy and bureaucracy?'

'Yes,' said John as he sank back into his tattered armchair, 'that is the position. Election promises are mere window-dressing. They are deceptions, quite deliberately planned to gull the electorate. The party heads have not the slightest intention of carrying out their promises. There is no planning in the normal sense of the word. All decisions are taken to tide over some crisis or other, not to anticipate the crisis and avoid it. Look at the part of the world you know so well. You don't tell me that this chaos in Kenya was unavoidable. It has arisen simply because the government hadn't the guts to declare firmly, 'You, the Africans, will have a larger say in the running of the country as and when you prove fit to shoulder responsibility, and not before. We are not going to give way to threats. We are not going to stand by while the economy of the country is sabotaged. And it will do you no good to go bellyaching to the Yanks or Russians. The change must be planned, gradual, and flexible. But, of course, they have given way to threats, and having sown the dragon's teeth they will now reap the harvest of corruption, violence, massacre, and bankruptcy.'

John and I spent many interesting hours swapping views on world affairs. But day after day passed without either of us receiving replies to the many advertisements we answered for jobs. And then one morning, in the early winter, I had a letter from a man in Fulham who said he would like to see me about helping him to run an import-export agency. It would be a part-time but 'the prospects are formidable'.

I called. I found him in a large stuffy room on the third floor of a dilapidated Victorian mansion. He turned out to be an Iraqi, but a Roman Catholic. Dark complexion, hawk-like nose, slow and deliberate in his movements, he pointed to hundreds of files lined up round the skirting boards and under the bed, and said in broken English, 'Everytink from Japanese ball-points to ice machines . . . sixpence to thousands of pounds.' He offered me some Turkish coffee and a fat untidy hand-rolled cigarette. He would pay me 5/- an hour for three hours twice weekly and 10% commission on anything I sold. He wanted no references, saying majestically that he was well able to judge a man's character on sight. I accepted.

As Mr. Hassan was an Oriental I suddenly thought what a fool I had been to accept the wage offered instead of haggling, so I said casually, 'Mr. Hassan, you will of course refund my fares.' This provoked a friendly argument, two more cups of coffee, a cigarette, and half an hour's debate on the situation in the Middle East. But I won my point and gained face. And by the end of this first encounter I had persuaded him that my

French was better than his English and to save mistakes we had better conduct our affairs in French.

Mr. Hassan had a brand new portable typewriter. His printed letter heads were in English, French and Arabic. He paid me each time by cheque, and as he wrote the whole in Arabic as well as in English, and required me to sign a receipt in both languages too; this exercise added fifteen minutes to my stint.

When I arrived for my three hours work I would find a pile of hand-written draft letters to firms in Syria, Lebanon, Iraq, Persia and Pakistan, scrawled on the inside of old envelopes ripped open and folded flat, on pieces of brown paper, on the backs of letters from Costa Rica, Nicaragua, and Guatamala. 'Yours of the 5th inst., to hand with grateful thanks . . .' 'We thank you for your favour of the 12th ult . . .' 'Looking forward to your kind acceptance of our quotation . . .' I objected vehemently and successfully to such prostitution of the English language. Yet what defeated me was how he justified an air mail postage account that must have totalled at least £4 weekly without the semblance of an order or commission payment. His business was as mysterious as he was easy-going and hospitable.

When I retailed the afternoon's events to John Grierson he blew out a huge cloud of pipe smoke and said : 'Sinister, Walter; sounds murky to me. However thirty bob plus fares is better than a kick in the pants, but keep it dark or you'll be on the carpet with the N.A.B. for trying to help yourself.'

There came an afternoon in mid-December when Mr. Hassan said he was tired and would have a snooze while I did the letters. He assured me the noise of the typewriter would not disturb him. He smoked a cigarette and soon fell asleep. The tap-tap-tap of the keys did not disturb him, but his snoring and peculiar hissing produced a crop of mistakes in my typing. Now and again I watched the sleeping colossus. An enormous paunch heaved and sank. His half-open mouth twitched, and now and again a beatific and rather silly smile passed over his swarthy face. Two hours passed. I had written about fountain pens from

Yokohama, cotton goods from Barcelona, printed silks from Benares, and refrigerators for Mexico and Jordan. And then, like a patient coming to after an anaesthetic, he gazed about him surprised and seemingly shocked that the room had not changed and I was still writing letters. But his exquisite manners quickly overcame any thoughts of grumbling.

'Such wonderful dreams,' he burbled stickily in French, 'wonderful dreams of Cadillacs, and diamonds and gold, of beautiful girls, blondes and brunettes, and marble baths and delicious perfumes.'

I said I often dreamed too but I never dared go to sleep again, for invariably I had a hideous and exhausting nightmare. 'Would you care to join me in some kebab,' he asked politely and tottered towards the bathroom, which adjoined his bedroom-cum-office. I accepted with pleasure. And while he cooked the rice and grilled the skewered meat over the gas-ring I typed three more letters.

He turned out a most appetizing meal, and to round things off he hauled out from under the bath a glass jar of green figs in syrup, the like of which I had not tasted since the war. Then he wrote out my cheque and receipt, saying that he was too tired to wash-up. Everything could stay until the morning, but we would have some coffee and a cigarette.

On this occasion he did not roll the cigarettes. He handed me a packet of Players saying, 'I expect these are more to your liking.' And from his pocket he produced a small paper packet and gave it to me. 'These are very special,' he smiled, 'take them home with you, and I promise that if you smoke one or two before you go to bed you will not have nightmares. They calm the nerves.'

On the way up to my room I noticed that John Grierson's light was still on. I knocked.

'Where the hell have you been?' he asked.

'With my oriental pal. I had dinner with him.'

'Any Circassian slaves?'

13

'No . . . at least not yet. They may visit us tonight.'

John eyed me suspiciously.

'Try a really good eastern cigarette for a change,' I said, and offered him one of Mr. Hassan's eight 'specials'. Tom held it up to his nose. 'Seems vaguely familiar,' he said, 'but I think I'll pop into bed before lighting up. It might be safer.'

For some months past I had had a regular routine last thing at night . . . my three lots of tablets for nerves, ulcer, sleeping . . . and the Evening Standard Word Game which I usually finished before falling asleep. But tonight there was the added anticipation of sleep without terrifying dreams. And contrary to my own rule I smoked in bed.

I remember nothing until 7.30 the next morning when I heard the slop of water and the scouring of a scrubbing brush below my window. It was Friday, the morning the landlady 'did' the front steps for the week-end. I felt drowsy and fell asleep again, but I did not dream.

John came to my room just after ten.

'It must be twenty years since I smoked hashish,' he said with a laugh, 'and I think your Iraqi friend ought to be paying you more than five shillings an hour for cloaking his nefarious activities. I should think the police would be most interested, and I'm jolly sure your Mr. Hassan would cough up quite a few shekels in hush money.'

'Never,' I replied, 'I'm certainly not incorruptible, John, but if you think I'm getting mixed up with the police again and risk them turning on me you must be crazy.'

'Sorry, Walter. I forgot. But you're through with Hassan, aren't you?'

'I am. I shall just send him a very polite letter saying I'm no longer available, and leave it at that.'

John said, 'Reefers have a wonderfully humanizing effect for a time. Could you spare a couple for our pals at the N.A.B.?'

Once again I was back to where I began. I was no better off or more secure than when I left prison. Feeling utterly depressed

I set off for the Ninety-Nine, knowing that I would get more relief from Mrs. Tonkin than from all the bureaucrats in England.

She had not changed, but she glittered with ornaments, some real, others faked. She said it was 'just marvellous' to see me again, and why hadn't I called her on the phone.

'Because, Helen dear, I'm useless. I can do nothing for you now, or ever.'

'Now listen, Walter,' she said severely, 'you're not to talk like that. You must not let these people get you down. From now on I'm takin' you in hand. First, dear, what is it going to be ... whisky, gin and Italian, or a cocktail? All you have to do is to say, and I pick up the phone. It's as easy as that. And a couple of smoked salmon sandwiches?'

She was so kind I felt tears welling up. It was awful. I was ashamed that emotions had broken through what I thought had become steel plate.

The next Sunday I had lunch with her, alone in her tiny flat in Milan Street, Soho. It was on the second floor above an Italian grocers shop. For lunch we had oxtail soup flavoured with sherry, grilled salmon and fruit salad with fresh cream.

'How's Nancy getting on?' I asked while we were washing up after lunch.'

'Fine,' she answered, 'you didn't know she joined a touring company, did you, dear? They'll be away another eight months in Canada, then New Zealand, and Australia.'

When we had put the plates and dishes away Helen showed me the other rooms in the flat ... two small bedrooms each with a single bed, built in cupboards and dressing tables, pale green fitted basins, and carpets in french grey. It seemed so odd that her taste in interior decoration was so impeccable, while her personal dressing was outrageous.

'This must have cost you a packet,' I said.

'It did dear, but I don't owe a bob, and that's honest. The washing machine. T.V., radiogram, fridge and deep-freeze, all the glass and crockery and stainless cutlery ... the lot ... it's paid for.' And then she made a remark that nearly knocked me out.

'You're an educated man, Walter. I'm a nobody. But we're both human and we're both lonely. Will you do me a favour? There's nothing sexy about it and no funny business like with your Mr. Bagdad, I promise. Will you come and stay as my guest for as long as you like? I'm earning plenty, Walter. You'd have to pay no rent. You help yourself and cook what you like. You come and go as you please. You have your own key. And I give you a receipt each week for the rent you don't pay, for three pounds which is just about what those officials will swallow. And if they call they're welcome. You have your room and I have mine, and they can think what they like.'

For a moment I was paralysed, speechless, confused. And then as though driven by some *force occulte* I was holding her tightly in my arms, kissing her, kissing her cheeks, her neck, her lips, her golden curls, and both of us were crying as though we were children who had found home and safety after hours of terror in a crowd of strangers. Never have I experienced such a flood of emotions. Never would I have believed that a man and a woman, the one over sixty, the other over fifty, could revert to adolescence without the slightest warning. It was a situation that defied analysis. But was it utterly irrational? Compared with the hell we had both been through month after month, the cruelty of man to man we had both suffered so long, what did background, class, language, accent, education, matter?

For a split second I found myself looking for her motives, seeing myself as an elderly worn-out gigolo, and I cursed myself for putting into Helen Tonkin's mind thoughts that I knew had never occurred to her.

I told John I had found better quarters and left it at that. And a week later I was installed as the 'unpaying' guest of the woman to whom I had been introduced by the charlatan Mr. Gerrard, who little knew the vicissitudes I would go through before 'dear Mrs. Tonkin' and I again shared the same quarters.

The time had come for me to give my ulcer a chance of healing by supplying my stomach with food adequately masticated.
In prison I had had four teeth extracted because the waiting list
for fillings was nine weeks. The regulations of the Assistance
Board provide for a refund of National Health charges, but I
wanted to avoid letting the dentist know that I was on the 'dole'.

I explained my point of view to the N.A.B. on the phone. 'In
that case,' said the Clerk, 'you should pay your dentist the £5
from your weekly allowance, obtain the appropriate form and
receipt from him, bring both to us, and the £5 will be refunded
immediately.' It seemed simple enough. I made an appointment
to coincide with the day of my allowance was paid. My dentist
handed me a receipt on the back of which he had written
'dentures'. I asked for a form. He said I required no form. There
was indeed no form he could give me since the only other docu-
ment involved must be sent to the Ministry to enable him to get
paid.

At the Board's offices I went straight to the Cashier's hatch
and knocked on the shutter. Nobody answered. After twenty
minutes the shutter opened and a name was called out. I nipped
in with my receipt and asked for a refund.

'I can't deal with you without authority,' said the Cashier,
'you must give your name in and be interviewed first.'

Half an hour passed. I gave my name in and retired to the
bench. A Negro woman, suckling an infant, and a mulatto of
uncertain origin were my neighbours.

I counted the number of applicants. There were fifty-nine,
thirty-three non-white. My name was called out and I moved
briskly to a cubicle.

'What can I do for you?' enquired a clerk I had never seen
before.

I explained that I had been promised an immediate refund
and handed him the receipt. He examined it as though looking
for maggots and gave me a dirty look. Without saying a word he

vanished through some swing doors. I was left to imagine a huddle between several termites and the queen in the bowels of the earth. Quarter of an hour passed. I finished the Daily Telegraph crossword. A tall scrawny man with high cheekbones and florid cheeks confronted me. He did not sit down.

'Where is the form?' he demanded brusquely.

'My dentist says no form other than the receipt is required.'

'This receipt would never stand up in a court of law,' he shot at me. 'Somebody has altered this figure from a 'one' to a 'five'. I noticed he had my dossier under his arm. It included my prison sentence.

'Are you accusing me of forgery?' I demanded.

'I'm accusing you of nothing, Mr. Musgrave. I am merely stating a fact, that this figure has been altered.'

'And the inference is that from the information you have rooted out and which you hold under your arm that I did it,' I said angrily.

'I am handling public money,' he said.

'Mine among others,' I retorted, 'why the hell don't you call the police and then we'll all know where we stand. Just think what the Mirror would say, 'Ex-R.A.F. pilot gets damages for wrongful arrest'. Or 'Crichel Down again?''

'It is my duty to make enquiries,' he sneered, and vanished through the swing doors. I had a strong suspicion that my request for the department to honour its verbal promise had caused such a stir that I had provoked the queen of the colony to action. But who can unmask these anonymous 'workers'?

Scarcely had the inquisitor gone than a young man in winkle-pickers crept into the cubicle. 'A bloody liberty,' he said in a hoarse whisper, 'matter of fact I've been in the 'nick' too, guv'nor. But these bastards'll never let you forget it.'

He popped back the moment his interviewer showed up. Nearly a quarter of an hour passed before Torquemada reappeared. 'I am not sure whether we or your dentist owe you an apology,' he said with reluctance, 'but the matter is now in order. If you take a seat on the bench the Cashier will pay you very shortly.'

I wanted to say, 'You haven't heard the last of this,' but I held my tongue. What was the point of risking victimization and the reduction of my allowance?

At my next appointment the dentist said he had never had such an experience in all the years he had been handling National Health patients. 'But why they are gunning for you and why should they be impudent to me?' he asked with good humour.

The following week I sent Torquemada a post-card to say I had changed my address. I am now under the surveillance of a different office. Whether they have digested my dossier or not I don't know, but they treat me with courtesy, send my book of vouchers in good time, and don't bother me with visits.

Helen has helped me to reduce my intake of barbiturates and I enjoy a pipe much more than cigarettes. And if my book on Africa is accepted I shall buy Helen a Dauphine and show her that even at sixty one I can play a full part in running our strange but contented household.

*　　　*　　　*

What has imprisonment done in my case? It came near to wrecking my physical and mental health. On the other hand, it provided work for doctors, specialists, radiographers, physio-therapists, pharmacists, manufacturing chemists, nurses, and a swarm of civil servants. By putting me in gaol the magistrates confirmed the truth of Parkinson's Law, for I am one of thousands who have helped two warders, two coppers, and two clerks, to grow where one grew before. For nearly one year I was wearing clothes other than my own. For nearly one year I was being taught to appear to be as busy as a bee while in fact being as idle and useless as a sloth. I learned that the British can be as brutal and sadistic as Nazis and as savage as Africans. To realize that may be a gain or a loss.

I failed, because 'an old dog' cannot learn to perform new tricks, to speak other than 'posh' English. I cannot undo the long training I have had in saving time and materials, and in never letting a day pass without adding something new and useful to my store of information. I could never destroy my pride to the extent of being obsequious or of showing respect for human vermin whose very behaviour invited loathing and contempt. I was duly punished. The punishment yielded a crop of side-effects. Perhaps the most lasting is that my views on capital punishment have changed. I believe 'topping' poisons and brutalizes the whole British Prison Administration. The law as it stands is so anomalous that we can either advance with other countries to abolition or go back to Tyburn. The present situation is too ridiculous to satisfy even the English regard for compromise.

It may have been useful too to find out at first hand that the Affluent Society has a complex but not wholly admirable conscience. It will rise up in wrath and indignation at the knowledge of horses transported for slaughter from Eire to France or Belgium, but it will do nothing for the 9,000 men of its own family who, at this very moment are cooped up in conditions, that were they apes or guinea pigs, would cause a public outcry. For the victims of tyranny and earthquakes and hurricanes it will find money and work and political sanctuary. Yet it is well content to starve the Probation Service and to do nothing for first offenders turned loose on release from prison.

The British have accused the UN of using a double standard in the Congo. But they too habitually use two standards, discriminating against those of their own kinship in Africa, and punishing twice and even three times, for the same offence, those who have crossed the law in England.

Self-deception has become a national pastime. An ex-prisoner tells his story without adornment or exaggeration. He leaves the public to draw its own conclusions. But it is more consoling to assume that all 'jailbirds' are liars or have a chip, while the hierarchy is enlightened and progressive. 'Dixon of Dock Green' is a pleasant soporific. It makes no demands on the cerebral mechanism of the viewers, and who would not prefer a view of Derwentwater or Mevagissey to the monotonous stream of traffic down Mile End Road?

National self-deception has cost the British millions of lives and millions in money. They chose not to believe that Hitler and his gang were bent upon world conquest.

Of Communism, far more subtle and dangerous, are they any the more wary? In England perhaps 'yes', but not in Africa which is the key continent in the struggle for survival between the East and the West. The public is ruffled, but little more, by the rise in crime. But is it concerned to delve into the reasons and to pinpoint just where the Welfare State is failing?

Very recently a man who has some knowledge of prison affairs and is plainly sincere wrote, 'The fact remains that seven out of eight first offenders sent to prison for the first time do not return'. Does the end, if it is true, justify the means? What becomes of the other seven? No case histories exist for it is the practice to throw ex-prisoners onto the economic scrap-heap . . . a habit that seems oddly at variance with the teachings of Christ.

What I have written may seem bitter, destructive, and cynical. But I have not forgotten that month by month more and more men, women, and children are being shovelled into gaol. For them I am writing 'How to be a Good Prisoner.' It will be 'Everybody's Guide' on how to keep sane behind walls, how to avoid the wrath of warders and the sarcasm of governors, why it is futile to escape without long-term planning, and what action to take to obtain enough nourishing food and a change of clothing without undue expense.

In the meantime, the Post Office workers, among others, are preparing to subsidize a number of M.P's to represent their interests in Parliament. This development accords with the rules of the modern democracy of pressure groups where constituents are a side-issue. No doubt the police and the warders will soon have their nominees on the back benches.

It is high time that ex-prisoners had a look in. There are thousands of well-to-do citizens who have escaped the jaws of the Avenging Giant more by luck than good management or morality. Should they not show their public spirit by sponsoring the National Union of ex-Felons rather than by letting their hearts bleed for abandoned birds and flutter for the fate of leopards and lions under an all-African 'government'?

Charity, one is told, begins at home. In the case of the ex-prisoner does it begin at all?

HOSPITAL SENTENCE

By Colin Franklin

ANY awkward experience can be partly judged by manners which are learned in English public schools. In those places for about five years boys are supposed to accept pains of the body and spirit, to absorb them as parts of the form of their world without more protest than anyone would reckon manly. Though this is less intense than a hundred years ago, the idea spreads. I met an American professor lately whose sons had been sent to a boarding school in Wisconsin. 'Did they enjoy it?' I asked. 'Of course they didn't, but it made men of them.' And the point for this book is that suffering of a fairly severe kind gets accepted as part of the normal growth.

My illness was not painful, so I cannot write about pain. Between any who have suffered pain, and the rest who have not, there is a greater division than between those who have felt some form of imprisonment, and the others who have not. And no outsider can interfere or speak for them. That is a general rule, and a reason why this book is made from chapters by authors whose varied experiences qualify them to know what they say. It is particularly irritating, for instance, to watch the tolerance of one who never suffered the pain he forgives; as when somebody who was safely in England declares wide forgiveness for what the Nazis inflicted upon other families. But I am concerned with what is normal—or what seemed so to a young man. Perhaps

the great merit of Victorian public schools was that after enduring them almost anything came within the limit of normal experience. I suspect that the sorrow of death, to the dying man
and his relatives, is near to this worry about abnormality. Death
is normal, like illness and imprisonment, but not appropriate or
convenient in company; not anything to laugh about. This
nuisance of not laughing about certain subjects, is a guide to
abnormality. Many events, like visitors, could be more easily
received if they were expected.

I went to hospital when I was twenty-one, on a November day
seventeen years ago, with tuberculosis. That was at Haifa, from
a naval destroyer. I was away from active life for eighteen
months, then came away from hospitals and their routine and
went up to Oxford. Only by remote analogy can that find a
place in the theme of this book, among people who have known
Japanese prison camps, Nazi concentration camps, political
prison in Hungary. But while it lasted one never knew the term
of the sentence; and it was a form of imprisonment for that
time; and any kind of prisoner can share the theme of inquiry
into how thoroughly he ever gets released.

One is trained to care more for mind than body. Self-absorption
is acceptable if it means, for instance, a spiritual retreat. If it
means withdrawing to an establishment where people discuss and
think out the span and scope of physical illnesses, that would
seem a contemptible neurotic waste. At first sight, a hospital is a
poor kind of retreat. I remember reading a life of St. Catherine
of Siena, and it comforted me then to think that she prayed for a
six-weeks illness. I would also have envied her the clear limits
of her sentence. But hospital generally means a confinement to
physical care. If we had left ourselves to the competent people,
taken no notice of where we happened to be . . . but we did not.

A form of self-respect is needed in long illness, and perhaps—
this book may suggest it—in all kinds of imprisonment. One
has the impression, reading a book such as *Solitary Confinement*,
that Christopher Burney kept self-respect through his experi-

ence; and Paul Ignotus writes in *Political Prisoner* about conditions in which this quality might have seemed impossible—yet he made poems in the darkness, and preserved some fragment of the truth about himself which he respected. When I came to Jerusalem in an ambulance, to the army hospital on Mount Scopus, a silly phrase persisted : 'my mind will decay'. Not that there was such a fine mind, or that decay would have mattered. In this adolescent spirit, building frail bricks against the rush of self-absorption, I sent for the *Critique of Pure Reason* because I had heard it was one of the most difficult books to understand. Long red-ink notes about the nature of *a priori* knowledge and the categories are all that remain in my books or brain.

But the impulse was right. If a busy man gets a temperature and goes to bed for two days, and talks about his headache and receives a shop of flowers, all is well. Our trouble was living between monthly X-rays with two-day temperature and its small talk magnified, stretching out until concern grew serious and the careless interludes became like casual ailments. Waiting from morning to evening for a fall of temperature, got extended to the longer wait from one month to another for the improved X-ray. And if it had not improved, the month had been wasted. Nobody bothered to suggest what a St. Catherine chance we all had. The hospital never felt like the small retreat or university it might have been. They brought round wool and knitting, calling it occupational therapy.

This view, from those years, looks foolish now. If I came to a public ward of a bad hospital now, I should be in anyone's eyes a bit less of a child; which means I would watch T.V. with the others, read a little in the quiet times if it were easy, and write observant letters. But the image of respect would be there still— in letters, and effort to understand.

The idea of death was too remote to worry us. That was too many corners away from most of us. I looked forward to Oxford, and expected to get there. The crossing we wanted to make was not from death to life, for we were not condemned in any serious way, or sickness to health; but from pity to envy again. We wanted to be envied again, not pitied. Some self-portrait I had painted in the minds of other people, I could see, had been changed and wrecked like the picture of Dorian Grey. People were sorry for a naval officer. They came up the hill on warm winter afternoons to visit and bring flowers. Some of the visitors seemed to be people whose lives, even outside hospital, nobody would envy. They came to see us, I thought, so that we at least would envy them. On Mount Scopus one easily thought in Christian phrases, though I am a Jew. Mount of Olives and the Garden of Gethsemane were just opposite. There was an absent-minded padre who came to call on us with just one sentence, spoken in one breath : 'I was in the Garden of Gethsemane this morning and do you know the smell of violets was absolutely overwhelming.' I observed that all of us searched for greater sufferers, and were calmer for finding them; and that Christians were saved the search by having Christ, whom they had placed forever in the position of greater sufferer. Their own lives, in regard to suffering, were physically less than his pain on the cross and spiritually smaller than the burden of their sin which he always carried. This went to the heart of the poetry of suffering; with the exquisite humanity of Christ's own despair in crying from the cross 'My God, why hast thou forsaken me?' It brought sanction to despair and loss of faith.

This poetry of suffering only once came near me, and by chance. A friend from school was an officer at the School of Arabic Studies in Jerusalem and came up to see me most days. His were the only good visits—because he mocked me, borrowed money, and turned the afternoons into laughing holidays. He sometimes brought another student at the school, Alan Appleford, a New Zealander who settled at the other end of my room to talk nicely with the sad Indian officer (one of the few who had cause to worry about health) with whom I shared a room. These were well-balanced days. After they had gone I could lie back to watch sunsets over the Hills of Moab, hear trolleys rattling along corridors with supper and listen to the bark of dogs below in the villages. Occasionally there were shots and sirens from the direction of the city, and then one felt secure and far away. One midday my friend came back, very smart in officer's uniform and polished leather straps saying, 'Now I can meet the Zionists on their own ground. Alan was shot last night.' 'Badly hurt?' 'Killed, what did you think. I've come to identify the body in the mortuary here.' This was the nearest I came to the irony of suffering. The visitor who had come to talk with the sick, lay dead below them next day in the same building. That ought to have blown the nonsense away from subtle musings about the great greater sufferer, and the gap between pleasure and sympathy.

Aristocrats tend to turn up in a classless society. I notice in my working life now, for instance, an aristocracy of authors whose books have been paper-backed. In hospital the doctors had a system of grades for TB patients—grade three would mean staying in bed except for the lavatory, grade four could have a bath, grade five up for an hour and so forth. The high-grade patients were aristocrats, a kind of prefects. The comparison with school life was often near. We had to be weighed each week, and should have gained weight because in getting the illness we had probaly lost a stone or two. Two high-grade patients in charge of the weighing kept a chart of weights, and we all spent anxious mornings before that ceremony. It gave those two great power to direct the moods of the day by deciding what we weighed. And the smaller class-differences declared themselves in each gain or loss, sending us back to bed to think out what these meant. When the doctor came round he might change a grade here and there. To be left as before when one had expected to be up-graded was like staying back in the same school class when one's friends moved up. It was not long since I had experienced that also. But pleasure came with a new grade when it was granted. Walking along the corridor to wash, after staying in bed eight weeks while bowls were brought, one saw every pattern of sunlight on the mosaic floor. Beyond the passage a big room opened out on to a balcony, and from there we had a view of the Mount of Olives and below to Jerusalem, the towers and Dome of the Rock. More attractive than the city were cypress trees on the Mount of Olives, and the peaceful high walls of a monastery there. That was the life I wished for, though it might have been similar to the one I had got.

Visitors brought bunches of cyclamen and anemones from the hills, and a wild kind of ragged tulip. My days were quite disciplined, with a hundred pages of philosophy before lunch, visits in the afternoon, and chess or more reading in the evenings. Peace came dropping slow. It was disturbing to have the pattern interrupted—as when beds had to be pulled into the passage one evening for a film at the far end. At Christmas we dressed into uniforms again for lunch at a long table in the passage, and paper hats. Our doctor wore his paper hat with a difference, and as if his gesture were jolly for us all. He was our Headmaster at the school play. Then we changed back, at ease in pyjamas again. A small choir of nurses sang carols in the yard, wired to loudspeakers which reproduced them in every room. It was a warm sunny day, and from my radio I clearly heard the service from Kings College in Cambridge.

> Now I am nearer to Bethlehem
> But further in spirit than you who sing.
> Against the pale blue sky they sway,
> The cypress trees, on this fair day.
> Shapes on the hills are lost in blue,
> In squares on the chairs the sunlight falls
> And drops in folds to dry my towels.
> The pilgrims come and Jerusalem sings
> But O God lend my spirit wings
> To sing with you this winter day in Kings.

In the evening an Arab pedlar who used to come up to our rooms selling chocolate, appeared briefly and breathless with a sack of oranges—on the way to Bethlehem. He was so keen to be there, one could think a whole ceremony waited for the arrival of that pilgrim.

We went away in April, but long before that some thread of security after surviving the war had been cut. Anything might have cut it, but for me—very unimaginatively as I see now—the war had let it stay. Apart from any medical shock, I was attacked by the futile voices of officers discussing their futures.

'Only trouble is I've had an AP and they said it would clear up in six months. I've had eight months now, and it's not a scrap better than when it started.' 'Same with me. Trouble is, once they've taken your ribs out you're no bloody good for the rest of your life.' Tapping their cigarettes over the floor as they said this, throwing crumbs to the sparrows.

As a child my grandfather had given me a little Victorian book of advice for all occasions. It might have come to him as an oddity in a book auction. The advice for bad thunder, with the storm overhead, was 'You should pull your bed into the middle of the room and pray, remembering that our Lord hath said, Every hair on thy head is numbered.' I was realizing in hospital, rather late in the day, that our hairs are not numbered. It was a naïve moment to be thinking of it; when peace had returned after the Nazis, after the survivors had been saved from the camps.

There is no way to explain what turns out to be moving and upsetting. Not merely great music, but the corniest climax of a poor film causes tears. This moment of focus has little judgment or taste. Tragedy can pass it by, and a charwoman shopping can pierce it. The man in a bus with his evening paper relaxes with the news of the day's distress, consoling himself with the greater sufferers. One is generally obtuse in response to misery. But newspapers offer the casual unsorted events and every day needs its headline. Beyond the range of ingenuity of editors, their knowledge of appetite, outer events can be drawn into the pattern of tragedy which needs no detection or headline. Even if the eye is feeble in judging sorrow, and chooses its episodes with no taste, the sufferers know better though there may be nobody to watch them. The observers get put in their places from time to time by the performers. This has happened in our lives on a great scale.

Going to Holland for a holiday after the war and listening to people who had lived in Amsterdam while the Germans were there, or talking in Paris with anyone who witnessed the occupation and resistance, one found a barrier which could never be crossed. Nothing to do with lack of friendship, but simply that these people had endured experiences which I had not, that they had become changed as a result, with a knowledge I would never have, and a part of their world was private, shared among themselves; an area of fears and heroes, nothing to do with me.

This was not humiliating, but a fact to recognize. What we could assess, beyond the scope of news and events, was the effect of concentration camps upon people who did not go through them; the influence of Nazi occupation on British people, for instance, whose country was not occupied.

One influence might well have been the death of that kind of religion my grandfather's book of advice had represented : the thought that every hair of our heads is numbered, that any element of a personally protective God stays in our image of religious hope. It was not dead, because these hopes never die. Only the other day that nice old couple, the parents of Astronaut Glen, declared they were not too worried about their son's trip because they knew God would protect him. If any religious mind wants to suggest a religious meaning in the camps and prisons, it might be that God wished to show once and for all, before hydrogen bombs make it too late, that man protects himself alone and can look to God at his peril.

It is the prisoners, in one way or another, who stand for that period of emphatic suffering. Now, eighteen years after the Nazis were defeated, kinds of prison are nearer than war.

Nothing in my own experience is interesting here. I came through it safely of course, came back to England to a naval hospital and out to a private sanatorium. It was not a prison, but the parody of a hotel. We had plenty of food and behaved politely to each other. There were small tables in the dining room, for the patients well enough to be up and about, and we kept them as in a ship. My first evening, in warm late summer, a kindly elderly man rubbed his hands as we sat down and asked 'and is this your first visit?' It seemed a wicked question then, suggesting endless returns there and hinting I would never completely escape.

In the naval place there had been privacy of a sort, life among my own kind; but this elderly ease and submission were disagreeable. I had learnt to get out of that brown room in Portsmouth —to telephone, or wander among the rhododendrons, or hire a car and be driven into the Hampshire country, to White's Selborne—but here were seasoned old adaptable people. At tea next day they noticed me, I could see that, but didn't include me—except as a gossip for storage, the new patient, another greater sufferer among them. A white haired lady poured the tea. They were all Mr., Mrs., no first names. With tea and gentility went gossip about the others—Mr. Wellon, who had lost weight last week—where was he? Back in bed, someone said, for an AP. Mrs. Bird, gone home to Leeds, had she left for good? Oh no, coming back in two weeks time, she couldn't leave for good. Anyone know what's going to be done? 'Oh yes,' the white haired lady said pleasantly as if it were the weather, pouring another cup, 'Thora'.

That was the bad threat, the rib-removing operation, carried out under local anaesthetic and in several stages.

There was a cup by each high bed, for spitting, a thermometer and temperature chart. They collected the cups each morning for analysis, and we were supposed to take temperatures and make up the charts ourselves. Not staff shortage, I thought, but seniority—the recognition of status as convalescent patients, seniors with a sense of responsibility, who could be trusted with knowledge of temperature charts. In fact I hid my chart away and faked it morning and evening, never once daring the fear of a true reading. The mug was hidden too, in the pretence I had nothing to spit and offer for analysis. And I filled my chalet with flowers to make it look like my room and fumigate the hospital.

One settled there, as anywhere, and the round of tests and pauses went on. Ceremonies of weighing and privilege, baths and clothes, walking and dressing-gowns continued as in Jerusalem. I could never believe in the end of it, and relapse looked always more vivid than release. Somebody was there from a Japanese prison camp, recovering, enjoying the peace of this after that. He said he had learnt to see what people were really like, and that the way they behaved in freedom no longer convinced him or appeared interesting. It amused him to shock our nervousness and greet me, for instance, in the evening with 'My God you look ill'. At first this didn't seem funny and I told him off for treating a serious subject lightly.

Small pleasures and observations appeared, as in the Jerusalem hospital. It was the country of the Paston family, and I got the Paston letters from the library. I could go as far as their village in my walks, and came to know intimately the shore and a near village, Trunch. It was such a rich village, so much to see. I borrowed a fat local history. When visitors came, to drive me through the country and as far as the Broads, I asked them to go slowly through Trunch and look at it carefully—and they did so, but saw nothing, for Trunch was small and we were in and through in a flash. They wondered what I had wanted them to look at.

Christmas came, and I went with a friend to Norwich Cathedral where there was a carol service. We sat in the choir of the crowded building and I tucked a bag of tangerines under my chair. As the procession came up the steps singing, a tangerine rolled out of the paper bag across the stone and stopped there, so bright and untouchable, in their path. They took no notice, avoided it, sang above it. The tangerine stood for something, I thought—crude in that grey normal world, rolled out for exhibition among holy men—anyway a few days later I left, unable (so I thought) to put up with it any more. So I went to a Shropshire cottage and utmost kindness, in the snowy winter of 1947, when taking exercise meant prodding the road slowly with a stick until drifts of snow came up to the handle and I knew it was too deep to go on. Snow was so deep in the little garden, that sheep came down from the hill to have vegetables from our hands. Then suddenly an end of treatment, home and in May to St. John's College, Oxford.

I had been released and what interests me now is our separation from prisoners, wherever they are; and how to avoid it. It may be that we are the prisoners, making for ourselves a prison of the normal. That is where we try to dwell, building the fences against abnormality and comment. In its several aspects we could put down the walls and join the abnormal, sharing these qualities of prison or freedom. There are practical ways to achieve this.

The first concerns our fundamental response to abnormal or imprisoned people: shock and horror. The wounded or criminal man causes it, an ill friend can be responsible for it. Strange behaviour brings it. A deep fault may be the way we protect children from such experience. When they meet it later —when we meet it—there must then be shock, a sense of division and remoteness. This illness or wound or sin is the knowledge from which we were protected. I think it may be that we should stop guarding children from any knowledge of truth; that they are ready for it, and can accept it. Anyway, they must. And television, which has no X and A certificate, is starting a sensible tendency that way. Children in television houses cannot be protected from knowledge of the world in the old Edwardian way. They learn, see and take it in, sifting and preparing. An absolute advance. A parent thinks: 'They will have enough of it later. Let them enjoy something like innocence as children.' But they will suffer from the shock later, climbing out from all this innocence. Or they stick to the story of the world's innocence, hurting themselves for too long.

My theme is the link of abnormality between sickness and prison, which Samuel Butler and no doubt many others have observed. Sickness of body or spirit is punished equally by confinement and separation. It is convenient that the term sickness covers each aspect of this guilt, and that the prison punishment greets each of its forms. Children should enter hospital, to see how common are illness and death. They might be excellent and cheerful guests there, and would learn to come without feeling shocked. Perhaps they could visit in prisons too, though that is not part of my story.

The second prison solution, nearer to my own minor experience, is to recognize that we are body, flesh and bone; and if something falls on us we smash, and if the wrong virus takes charge we submit. Health is a temporary chance, not a right or splendour. The sermons are forever agreeing we are 'members, one of another'—and as so often, there is no better way of putting it; except that the phrase grows weak, and we forget what it means. I understand it partly to mean that we, the well, are Siamese twins with the sick. Visiting hospitals or prisons should not be a strange effort, for we belong in them. One part of me is sometimes outside, another part sometimes in. Prison and hospital are not further away than shops and fields—unless I take this particular physical moment to be my life.

From the other end of it, this assumption would make a lot of difference to prisoners and patients. Some of the envy and displacement would go, or worry them less. The irritant is not merely one man's isolation in cancer or torture, I suspect, but the longing to be back and normal where he belongs; forgetting that the 'normal' ones belong where he is equally. The psychoanalytic norm is probably as savage and philistine as that other which is accepted as a cruelty, the Stakhanovite. If nothing is normal, we cannot want so fiercely to get back to it. This is true to the smallest platitude of a child's ration of chocolate biscuits.

Professor Trevelyan once wrote that he thanked God for every change of weather; and that is sound advice down to the analogy of thanking God for torture; except that we have the marvellous protest on high authority, of 'Why hast thou forsaken me?' Without that cry, many people might have found Christianity less bearable.

It is common to be more sentimental than formerly about names and differences, more sensitive and considerate. As a child I used to see a hospital called 'St. Luke's Home for the Dying' as I came home each day from Kensington Gardens. It did not impress me much—they were dying, I not yet. Then it was changed to 'St. Luke's Hospital for Incurables'. That was a doubtful difference, a promotion which perhaps meant very little to the patients. They were not likely to be fooled by that name. Every home in the country, of course, is for the dying, only they were nearer death than most. It was a reasonable name in its first form.

A final possibility behind this book is that anyone coming out from forms of imprisonment can for the rest of his days have the pleasure of not being imprisoned. The question, as the editor phrased it, was: 'Does one ever get out?' And I doubt whether these negative graces ever last for long. The pleasure of losing a toothache lasts about twenty minutes, of coming ashore from a rough sea voyage rather longer. Nobody stays merry about these things, except by effort and intellect. A gap of fuss or worry has to be filled. Torture and hospital were bigger decays, drilled larger holes where ordinary distractions have to be packed in by time, the dentist. That is a clearer metaphor than to imagine there is any standard of normality which commands loyalty and affection among those who have been forced for a period to lose sight of it.

So the writers here who have travelled to the ends of fear, and returned, need not be envied. It does not mean that they know fear familiarly now, and forget it. Torture, illness, solitude are all tests which one may be ready for when they come or at any time, or never. Going through them perhaps makes little difference, except that one's character emerges and the results are known. For myself there was no new strength, but if prison or hospital were accepted as basic human rights there would be less fear about the thought of entering them.

TRUE MADNESS

By Jeremy Bryan

AUDIBLY a door is unlocked from within. It opens and a male nurse receives you from those who have delivered you. He closes the door behind you—and locks it again.

Not ostentatiously; but he locks it nevertheless.

Then, dispassionately, neither hostile nor friendly, he invites you to change out of your suit into the ward uniform of ill-cut clothes or pyjamas—because on these there there will be no belts or braces or shoe-laces with which you may strangle either yourself or others : hidden in them are no knives or razor blades with which to cut a throat.

He explains that you will be given a safety razor so that you may shave when necessary : and the careful casualness of his tone tells you at once that, when you do shave, you will be watched.

Having signed an inventory of your clothing and personal possessions, and having briefly seen the ward doctor, you are shown to your bed, and—as other patients survey you with eyes that are brightly curious, or darkly hostile, or blankly indifferent —you are told not to worry : just to co-operate and you will get on fine.

Not just to co-operate and you will soon get out; but just to co-operate and you will get on fine.

For this is neither a gaol, within which you are to fulfil a sentence, nor an ordinary hospital wherein you will, within recognizable limits of time, be cured. This is a psychiatric ward. And here your sentence cannot even be pronounced until you have proved yourself completely co-operative. And your cure— well, what's the use of talking about cures when no one yet knows why you are mentally ill? *'Cure'* is a grandiose word in psychiatric medicine. *'Cure'* is a giant step into a new world for the mentally very ill. And with only that infant of sciences, psychiatric medicine, to help you on your way . . . Well, let's not think about cures yet. Let's just suggest settling into the routine and co-operating.

Of this much will any patient be aware the moment he enters a ward for the more disturbed of the mentally ill. The rest he will—and must—learn as he goes along. By the time he is discharged, he will have learnt a great deal.

It is the first encounters—so inalienably removed from normalcy—that hurt the most.

The ward idiot (really an idiot? or just acting the idiot, in unco-operative revolt against the system? No one knows) who confronts the newcomer and, pointing to solid floor, scrupulously waxed, says: 'You just pushed me into that hole!'

How to deal with the idiot and his non-existent hole, but his seemingly real indignation about being pushed into it? . . . that may well be the novitiate's first ordeal. Should one make public his idiocy by retorting that there *is* no hole—and so perhaps risk more violent delusions? Or agree with him, and apologize, thereby becoming an accessory to his madness?

But what if *he* knows that in fact there is no hole there? Then, by agreeing and apologizing, you assume the mantle of a lunatic delusion peculiar, in the eyes of those who watch the scene, to yourself. And many are watching.

Mercifully one of them is almost certain to rescue you from your dilemma. Usually either an alcoholic, now almost cured, **or** an extrovert schizophrenic in one of his more stable moods.

Brushing aside the pot-holer, he will explain that this always happens, and introduce himself.

If he is an alcoholic he will, of course, quickly explain to you that alcoholism is why he is there. Snobberies exist even in psychiatric wards; and no self-respecting dipsomaniac wants to be confused with the rest of the herd who are manic depressives, pseudo epileptics, failed suicides, catatonics or unpredictable schizophrenics.

Since you have entered the ward on your own two feet it becomes instantly obvious to the pair of you that you are not helpless with the D.T's, and that, therefore, by implication at least, you too are being classed as one of the less desirables by the ex-alcoholic who has just introduced himself; but, since he has just rescued you, you accept the implication. And so, on your first day in the ward, you run the risk of accepting not that you are a human being who is ill but that you are a being, not altogether human, who is different.

The risk is even greater, however, should your rescuer be a schizophrenic. The sociable schizophrenic is often intelligent, always glad to see a new face, and frequently either an advocate of suicide or a pathological liar—or both.

Amiably escorting you to the sanctuary of your bed space, he will say : 'I'm a schizo; what are you?' And because at this stage you either don't know, or are not yet sufficiently brazen to declare it, this can be just as embarrassing as being confronted with a non-existent hole.

But the moment will pass because the schizophrenic is keener to talk about himself than to listen, although clever enough, often, to camouflage this fact by talking mainly in questions.

'Did you try to commit suicide? That's why you're here? . . . No? Well, that's why I'm here. Cut my wrists. Look.' He shows purple scars on his wrists. 'But my wife found me and rang the ambulance. You married? . . . Well, you'll see her on visiting days. My wife's all right. But cold, you know? She found me the time before too. I took rat poison then. They used the stomach pump on me. You ever had a stomach pump? ... No? Well, anyway, next time I'm going to jump under a train. See that fellow over there? He jumped under a train. He's a schizo too. Withdrawn though. Won't talk. The train only cut his arm off. What were you outside? A pilot, eh? I flew Spits in the Battle of Britain . . .' And so on.

And later you will discover that he also fought as a Commando in Italy; was a prisoner of war in Korea; studied medicine in Edinburgh, economics at London and drama at R.A.D.A.—has done everything that anyone else ever did, and a great deal more besides; and—for all that he looks to be only twenty-eight—must be at least a hundred and nineteen years old to have accomplished so much.

For the moment, though, you know only what he has told you, and are vaguely disquieted by the calmness with which he accepts his own aberrations. But at least he is some point of contact in this world full of strangers.

He will almost certainly escort you to your first meal (no knives allowed) and, excited by the presence of a listener who does not know the truth about him, tell many more lies in his anxiety to impress, to make a friend.

Overlooking, of course, that at his other elbow, and across the table from him, sit people who do know the truth. Inevitably then, as he tells you about his exploits as a Spitfire pilot, someone will taunt:

'Thought you were too young for World War II? Thought you were a p.o.w. in Korea?'

'I was sixteen when I flew Spits. Put my age forward,' he will insist: but anxiously, for he knows that he is trapped; knows what is coming.

'Of course he wasn't a p.o.w. in Korea,' someone else will contradict; but in conspiracy. 'He was a Commando in Italy! Weren't you, feller? *After* you flew Spits.'

'Sure. I was grounded after I pranged so I joined the commandos.'

'And then studied medicine at Edinburgh.' Someone else joins the baiting.

'And economics at London.'

'And acted with Larry.'

'I did *not* act with Larry. I studied at R.A.D.A.'

'When you were thirty-eight?' incredulously.

'When I was twenty-four.'

'But you said you studied at R.A.D.A. three years ago.'

'So I did.'

'Then you were thirty-eight. You were eighteen when you flew Spits in 1940 . . .'

'I was *sixteen!*' desperately he shouts.

'So in 1963 you must be forty-one . . . .'

'I'm twenty-seven.' Now he is roaring. At which everyone laughs.

'In that case you flew Spits when you were four years old,' his tormentors tell him. 'What a precocious child you were.' But the last jibe is wasted. Already your friend has fled the scene of battle; fled to the safety of his bed. Only he is not any longer your friend. You and he both know that.

After the meal, most of the patients will withdraw to the recreation room. There are newspapers to be read, or torn up by anyone sufficiently distracted; television to be watched, or studiously ignored by those few who are always fearful of the secret beams emanating from its cowboy embattled screen; and ping pong to be played.

Ping pong, indeed! Long after you have recovered and been discharged from this ward and gone back to your normal occupation, and forgotten even what the pot-hole idiot looked like, you will remember the sound, interminably repeated, of celluloid ball hitting wooden table and then corked or sand-papered bat.

On the whole, patients play listlessly. Not badly. They had had too much practise to play badly. But listlessly. They play it at all only because it fills in a bit of time and because not to play is a sign of unco-operativeness.

You see, the nursing staff watch you all the time. They have to, for their own and their patient's safety, of course. Most especially they must watch the suicide cases, for each of whom, in the office, there is a red card. When the staff come on duty they read the details on all the red cards and sign them, and so become responsible for watching the patients concerned incessantly and preventing them from further attempts on their own lives.

But they also watch the rest of you to see whether you are cheerful and industrious. You can be cheerfully industrious—as normal people are—during the day by making your bed with a smile, by helping clean the ward with a whistle, by washing up after meals without protesting. You can be cheerfully industrious in the evening by helping with the distribution of drugs—of vile tasting, evil smelling peraldehyde, of tranquillizers for the excitable and sleeping pills for the sleepless.

But in the Recreation Room you can only prove yourself cheerfully industrious by reading any newspaper or book not yet torn up by the distressed; by watching cowboys do battle on the television screen; or by playing interminable games of ping pong.

Which you had better, therefore do : because if you don't, the staff will be compelled to note down, in their day-to-day record on each patient, that you are 'unco-operative'. And the psychiatrist, observing this, knowing that he has not available to him a hundredth of the time he needs for the analysis even of those who *are* co-operative, will postpone his first appointment with you. And until his first appointment with you, there can be no treatment : until treatment, no medically accepted improvement : until improvement, no discharge. Oh yes—by all means play ping pong.

After that, a mug of tea or cocoa : then drugs for those on treatment : then bed for all. Your first night in bed among the mentally ill.

But your fellow inmates are surprisingly restful : or not surprisingly, if you understand about the drugs they have been given. Soon you sleep, almost unaware of the constant watch on all of you; almost forgetting the indignity of that locked door and the barred windows.

And then, abruptly, frighteningly, you are awakened. All around, darkness : but a gloomy figure, male and white-clad, is whispering at you.

'Fill this,' he orders, without explaining why, and offers what turns out to be a urine bottle. Apparently half-way through your sleep is the best time to get the best samples for urine tests : but no one has thought to warn you of this. Once again, as you first were by the pot-hole idiot, you are given notice of the fact that you are now in the hands of a new system, none of whose rules are known to you. Yet already you are aware that to break any of these rules is dangerous. It will mark you down as unco-operative. You go to sleep again reconciled to the idea of keeping close to your fellow patients so that you may do as they do; and only if you are exceptionally perceptive will you realize that, by so doing, you run the even greater risk of infection by the contagious and despairing neuroses which are theirs.

Up early in the morning, you make your bed, accept the safety razor that is offered to you, wash and shave under supervision, and eat your breakfast. Your schizophrenic friend is silent and sullen. No one takes any notice of him. And the room is not as full as it was at supper time. When you ask why, it is explained that the E.C.T's don't have breakfast. And when you ask what E.C.T's are, you will be told : 'The people on Electro Convulsive Therapy. Shock treatment.'

The older and crueller hands will then horrify you with stories of the obscenely convulsive reaction caused by this shock treatment when they had it, omitting to explain that nowadays it is administered under an anaesthetic and is positively enjoyed by many who undergo it. However, *their* horror stories will evoke other horror stories.

Ex-alcoholics will claim that shock by insulin treatment is worse, the patient being lashed into his bed and insulin injected to consume all the sugar in his blood, pitching him, in a wild but scientifically controlled plunge, towards death. And then, at the last moment, by pouring glucose into him, the blood's sugar content is restored with dramatically abnormal speed, and he is hauled full speed from death's depths to life's surface. Shuddering, gasping, clawing and convulsing, the patient returns to consciousness.

'Suffering,' the old hands will claim, 'from acute emotional bends! Like divers—only it's mental.'

'But that,' someone else will claim, 'isn't half as painful as that asphyxiation shock treatment'—and will tell how gas was administered to him until he almost died for want of oxygen and then was over-swiftly revived with oxygen.

All of these were treatments aimed at restoring, by shock, a degree at least of emotional stability to the emotionally unstable; all of them are now discredited, no longer employed.

But it is not encouraging to hear that only seven or eight years ago they were employed, and hopefully employed. Horror methods with horror results—all now abandoned. How many of today's methods, having been discredited, will likewise be abandoned seven or eight years hence? Will what they propose doing to you be just as barbaric as shock by gas, or by Insulin, or by electricity without an anaesthetic? To the surprises of the system under which you now live is added the element of terror. Who *are* these people who control you today? Anxiously you examine them afresh.

And in them observe no signs of brutality: but none of any warmth either.

In fact they are carefully good-natured in their behaviour, even if, behind their masks of patient acceptance as normal of pot holes, obscenities, hysteria and imbalance, there lies a wariness. Not the wariness of a prison guard alert against carefully planned attack and escape; but the wariness of nurses whose charges, without warning or plans or even being able to help themselves, may become violent.

Equally, though, these are not nurses of the type found in

any other hospital ward, for here the usual patient-nurse relationship is impossible. Here there can be none of the dramatic and rewarding struggle which exists elsewhere as a patient is nursed through a potentially mortal crisis and back to health.

In mental illnesses, cures are not dramatic, but imperceptibly and tediously slow. A hand that is gentle and soothing to one can hardly be expected to overpower and put in a strait-jacket another. And anyway, in cases of acute mental illness, the only relationship that theoretically matters is that which will exist when the patient accepts the psychiatrist as a father figure.

In ordinary wards, nurses are the stars and doctors are guest artists. In psychiatric wards, the psychiatrist is the star, the patient is his supporting actor ... and the nurses play only bit parts. They perform competently, without either gentleness or rancour. Whilst fully prepared to combat deterioration, they expect no rewarding miracles of healing. At best they hope for reasonable calm—and co-operation : at worst they are prepared to exercise the violence of the strait-jacket or the padded cell, and to contemplate, without anguish, a patient's certification.

It would be an unusually wise patient, however, who appreciated all of this on his first day in a psychiatric ward. He will much more likely decide that his male nurses are heartless brutes, that the whole system of locked doors and discredited horror treatments is medieval, and that a wicked injustice has been perpetrated upon him in ever confining him here.

Should you so decide, though, you will be left little time to brood upon your discontent. The ward must be swept, the breakfast dishes must be washed, those to be interviewed by the psychiatrist must be warned ... and the remainder must be kept occupied.

It is this latter which, unless you are of a disposition so placid as to be almost moronic, will, in the weeks and months that follow, more than anything else, tend to drive you truly mad : for every day, even though you are passionately unenthusiastic, you will be required either to weave or to carpenter or to paint or to work metal. At the very beginning of your illness you may actively dislike most of these splendid occupations : but you will have to practise at least one of them daily, and by the end of your treatment you will actively detest all of them.

Of the lot, weaving is perhaps the least distasteful : so let us assume that you will weave. Amiably instructed by your Occupational Therapist, you will tie what seem to be a million threads on your loom, learn to understand its primitive mechanism and then begin the interminable shuttling and banging, allegedly therapeutic, which goes towards the weaving of a scarf. That this scarf will turn out to be so raggedly unattractive that not even a tramp would wear it is not allowed to deter you from weaving it any more than it does your supervisor from making you.

'Watch your selvedge,' the Occupational Therapist will chide occasionally, as well (noticing the embryo scarf's jagged profile) she might; so you try to beat more evenly. And you begin to hate the loom, and the scarf, and the Occupational Therapist, and the whole system behind it all, with a hatred of quite venomous frightfulness. But you will continue to weave throughout the entire period, or receive an adverse report from those in charge, which is an even worse fate than weaving.

Thus the days will begin to pass, and to achieve a pattern. You will learn to ignore the ward idiot and to avoid pushing him into holes. You will learn the full details of each suicide attempt by each of the failed suicides. You will sympathize with the man who first took psychiatric advice because suddenly, and quite without reason, he developed a fear of eating lest he choke, or of shaving lest he cut his throat, or of travelling in a bus lest he suffocate . . . and is now, after long months of treatment, inclined to burst into tears at the drop of a hat . . . and is quite mad.

You will learn not to be appalled by the pseudo epileptic who throws regular tremendous fits, threshing and foaming : but only when there are people around him, never when he is alone. He wants attention. Electro-encelphelographs have proved that he is not an epileptic : the overwhelming desire for attention makes him behave like one. You will soon cease to be outraged by the indifference with which both staff and patients treat his melo-dramatic attacks; although perhaps each time he has one, your heart will lurch a little at the thought of anyone being so insecure that he must seek sympathy and attention in this manner.

You will finish one scarf, and promptly start another. You will see the psychiatrist come and go; and wonder why he never calls *you* into his consulting room, because, having seen so much true madness now, you know that he need only talk with you the once to appreciate instantly that *you* do not belong here. But, day after day, he will not call you in.

And daily the hero of the Battle of Britain and Anzio and Korea, the bright boy of half-a-dozen Faculties and of R.A.D.A. itself, will become more sullen. Like the pseudo epileptic, he too craves attention : but, unlike the pseudo epileptic, there are no limits to the means he will employ to obtain it.

Thus one day he will refuse to weave, or to make his bed, or in some other manner to conform. He might even start a fight or attempt to drown himself in the lavatory bowl. He will do something any way aggressively unco-operative; and so will ob-tain his passionately desired attention.

Unfortunately, however, it will not be the kind of attention his fellow patients want him to obtain, for again, unfortunately, but of necessity, unco-operativeness of this kind attracts stern measures from the staff; and stern measures imply defeat to the hero; and defeat is unheroic.

At which he fights back. And is man-handled into a strait jacket, where, physically incapable of impressing anyone any longer, he will start to scream as he is locked in isolation in a padded cell. Now will begin the time that patients hate as much as the staff.

Except for moments of silence caused by exhaustion and the few hours of it ensured by a hypodermic needle, he will scream unceasingly for days and nights on end. Then ward tensions will mount : other schizophrenics, in their hatred of the screaming hero, will announce coldly that *all* schizophrenics should be put permanently to sleep : the idiot's holes will grow deeper and more numerous; the pseudo epileptic will throw three fits a day : the man who fears food lest it choke him will starve : the staff will be doubly watchful and not half so good-natured : the Occupational Therapist will make you weave more industriously than ever.

Until, abruptly as it all started, it ends. The hero collapses and sleeps it off; the ward and the patients relax; and the whole cycle starts again.

This time, however, it will start with a faintly different *motif* —as if a well known play were being reinterpreted by a new producer. The script and plot will be the same, the motivation different.

This time, because of the crisis so recently past, those suffering from severe anxiety neurosis, who have doubtless been most distressed by the uproar of the last few days and nights, will be more resentful than hitherto of schizophrenics. Equally, the alcoholics will become more disdainful of all the other inmates : and the E.C.T's will tend to become resentful of all the non-E.C.T's : and those who feel wrongly confined and want only to go home will show frank contempt for those (not necessarily the minority) who fear discharge and would prefer the security of the ward to be made permanent. In the next few weeks, though the dialogue will be as it has always been, it will have subtle nuances of hostility.

It will also have, to continue the stage metaphor, different lighting. To the previous clean-cut spotlight of clinical care will be added a dozen deep blues and odd pools of shadow, all establishing firmly the latest ward mood of failure. Failure upon the part of the patients, which mainly is why they are there : failure on the part of the staff, which is why their patients stay there. More sombrely, then, and probably less confidently, you, the newcomer, will enter the second cycle of your stay.

This will be marked mainly by the beginning of your treatment; and by the feeling that nothing is any longer predictable.

You will visit the psychiatrist at last, expecting vague disapproval. Instead, he will invite you to take a seat and to have one of his cigarettes; and he will assure you that everything you tell him, though he makes notes of it, will be completely confidential.

Of course you are not to know that the smoothly offered seat and cigarette are a formula, for putting you at your ease, as trite as Dale Carnegie's for making friends. Nor are you to realize that the confidential notes are seldom locked away and are frequently read, strictly for amusement, by the nursing staff. Instead, you take your seat, you light one of the psychiatrist's cigarettes and you begin to answer his questions.

Under his analysis you must be as undeterred by his concentration on the more sordid aspects of your past life as he is impassively determined to show no surprise at, for example, your being in love with a nanny goat. The rules are that, just as no answer is allowed to shock the psychiatrist, so no question may outrage the patient. And even if it should seem to you that you are obliged to endure many more outrageous questions than the psychiatrist is required to hear shocking answers, that does not alter the rules.

Anyway, the whole process is rather a waste of time because this same psychiatrist, if he were in private practise, would never dream of hoping to complete his analysis and to cure you in less than a year of weekly meetings. In the ward, however, he will see you once a month, if you and he are lucky . . . and neither he nor you want to remain in the ward for four years.

No, he only hopes to get close enough to your problem to prescribe the right treatment to keep you reasonably stable and wholly co-operative; and the rest is up to you. Having seen him, you will return to ward life; to brooding, impending crises, and to some drugs or treatment which previously you have not received.

You will also have your blood tested, your brain's impulses

recorded, your spontaneous reaction to test words examined in
the light of your confidential utterances to the psychiatrist, and
your impressions of Rorschach's coloured blots analysed. You
will also realize that you are embarked upon a long course of
confession to sins and weaknesses you knew not ever to have been
yours.

Meantime, you will grow accustomed to the supervised bath
night (no chains on the bath plugs lest you hang yourself whilst
a male nurse has his back turned), to the issue on bath nights of
clean underclothing; to the dotty clergyman whose manners are
impeccably Christian, whose appetite disgusting and whose
present appointment (allegedly) is that of personal Chaplain to
Her Majesty the Queen; to the ward friendships and antipathies;
to everything, in short, except the accursed weaving of scarves
and the futile passing of days in which no one, from nurses to
doctors, ever says that the day of your discharge comes closer.

At this stage it is easy, just as you have lost your terror of treatment, to lose your confidence in its efficacy. No one ever really
seems to get better. And the visitors who come on visiting day
do seem so terribly *sane* compared with the inhabitants of your
ward.

Actually, they also seem terribly sane to most of your fellow
patients, with the result that, on visiting days, you all become
ashamed of one another. So you avoid introducing your nice
sane friends from outside to your friends who are shameful, because insane, inside. And they don't introduce their visitors to
you. Before visiting day you may all have assured yourselves that
you are just patients in hospital, like any other patients in
hospital : but on the day itself, it doesn't work.

Somehow the paranoiac patient with his broken mind can't
feel the same sort of complacent invalidism on visiting days as
the orthopaedic patient with his broken legs. For one thing, you
can't set a broken mind in plaster and suspend it impressively
from a pulley : for another, even if you could, the world (both
visitors and inmates) still can't accept the injured mind in the

jolly 'brought-you-some-grapes' fashion with which it accepts a maimed or infected body. To add to the ordeal of avoiding any introductions to your fellow patients, there is all the time the uncomfortable knowledge that your visitors (your reaction to them and theirs to you) is being watched. Your wife or mother or son might even be discreetly called aside and lured into the psychiatrist's consulting room, to face questions complementary to those asked from you. Complementary and just as awful. When it happens, you sit feeling lonely and treacherous, remembering your hateful confessions, wondering what horrible further evidence is at this very moment being gathered for use against you. Then your visitor returns to you—and you both, self-consciously, talk trivialities till it's time for non-patients to leave. As you say goodbye, you may even feel relief : not that nothing between you has been made explicit, but that the visit is over, that any second now you will be back in the world you know— of head cases !

Here, of course, is where the worst menace of such wards lies. Here nothing you do because of your illness is going to shock anyone. Here there will always be someone more cracked than yourself; and no one so wholly stable that he may despise your instability. Even the staff may not despise your instability, because you know that they are paid not to. And your fellow patients tell you that most of *them* will eventually go off the deep end anyway. So here, among the unstable, you feel safe : and your unaccustomed sense of safeness can easily induce an apathy, if not a hostility towards the idea of ever being discharged from it. Especially since cures seem to take so long; if, in fact they can be achieved at all. Why sweat out dozens of demoralizing interviews with the psychiatrist in the dim hope of a discharge into the uncertain world of normalcy, when you can relax, drifting apathetically in the ward's soothing tide of fellow-sickness, and, forever undischarged, feel quite safe where you are?

Why make the effort to get back to the routine grind of a job, and family responsibilities, and the world's problems, and the income-tax man's demands? Here you can't be sacked, sued, attacked or taxed. And you will be fed, clothed and occasionally entertained in return merely for making your bed, bashing out scarves and co-operating over the ping pong table. When you are mentally ill, the bargain seems treacherously attractive.

More often than not, though, something happens which, at the last moment, will stop you surrendering. It may be that the drugs prescribed for you have sufficiently muted your excitability, or boosted you in your black depression, to let you realize how terrifyingly and much more ill are most of your fellow patients. Appreciating their problems, or delusions, your own seem suddenly less.

Or it may be that one day you find yourself vitally concerned with the future safety of the suicide patients whom you have heard conspiring, on their discharge, to kill themselves. Or genuinely amused by the pot-holer when he enters into a furious argument with the gluttonous Royal Chaplain, the latter denying the former his holes; the former denying the latter his Palace appointment.

Then you will begin to mend, cured more by pills and the extremes of your fellow sufferers than by any too brief analysis or psychiatry.

The staff will observe your increased cheerfulness and stability : the psychiatrist will examine your dossier with more hope—and possibly suggest pentathol, under which you will get everything off your chest that he hasn't already prised loose.

Lying on a bed in his consulting room, you will watch him tie the rubber pad round your upper arm and slip a needle into a consequently distended vein. Or is it artery? You don't care much anyway because now he has loosened the restricting rubber pad and the pentathol is surging through you and you're suddenly exquisitely drunk and couldn't give a hoot in hell about anything.

You know he's sitting beside you and about to ask dozens of revoltingly personal questions, but, if he wants to ask them, why should you worry? And so he asks them : and, mildly astonished, you hear yourself answering with fearful candour.

Sometimes you feel he's gone a bit too far, even for a psychiatrist, and you equivocate. You don't lie, because that takes an enormous effort and you really can't be bothered with enormous efforts : but you can equivocate. And even then you know that, by pausing, you have told the psychiatrist that you're equivocating. But why should you care that he can work the rest out for himself? Next question, please!

Slowly, but quite agreeably, all the unspoken and most of the unspeakable things are extracted from your pentathol-liberated mind. Then you sleep.

When you wake up, you will know that soon, in a month or two, you will go home. It will have to be a month or two both because the psychiatrist has to be certain or your recovery and because he's got quite a few others to examine before he can take another look at you. In the meantime, back to the routine; the only change being that now you won't dread visiting days and will even shamelessly introduce your dear sane visitors to your dear dotty friends in the ward. You may even introduce them to the idiot, because no one ever comes to see him; and when he promptly repays you by accusing your visitors of having pushed him into a hole, you will feel no embarrassment at all.

Then the strength of your new-found stability will be tested by the inevitable crisis in the ward's immutable emotional cycle. Once again someone will start a row, be clapped into a padded cell and, dog-like, begin to howl. Because of the darker motivation from which this second screaming bout has arisen, it will probably be a worse bout; and it may even induce a second collapse into insane baying. With two of them howling and shrieking and roaring, you will need all of your recently acquired sense of humour and compassion to survive.

They will howl together in chorus, they will howl in turn, they will howl as if in conversation; and they will howl in violent competition.

Naked and demented they will rage round their padded cells, defecating shockingly and screaming insults at those in the ward beyond. They will scream your name. They will name your mental illness. They will spit obscene drops of verbal venom into every nearly healed wound of your convalescent mind. They will know that you are getting better and, resenting it, will fight dirtily and cunningly to drag you back into their own hopeless depths. And you will either crack and sink, or you will rise above it and wonder how you could ever so nearly have been as they are.

You will admit frankly that once you *were* almost as flawed in your mind as they now are in theirs: but you will wonder how this could ever have been. Consoling the man who is afraid of eating, and who now, under the appalling stress of the animal shrieks beyond, cries almost continuously, you will realize that the world of the ward is not any longer your world. Lifting the pseudo epileptic back on to his bed (for he has convulsed himself a little too much and thrown himself onto the floor) you will look forward to paying more attention to others outside.

And so comes the day when you are given back your own clothes—even, if you brought one with you, your own razor— and are ready to go home. You will shake hands with your ward friends. You probably won't see any of them again, because the best thing for all of you is to forget each other and get on with life: but you will be grateful to them: and either glad because there is hope for them or sad because their cases are hopeless.

You will shake hands with the staff, suddenly pleased that they remained always detached when you were ill, because now that you have recovered you can say goodbye to them as equals. You will thank the psychiatrist ... and appreciate for the first time that he is harassed and overworked and as humanly fallible as the next man; that the frightful confessions you have made to him will fade completely from his mind almost at once as, impassively, having offered a seat and a cigarette, he listens to the confessions, equally frightful, of those who remain in his care.

A last wave, and you will be at the front door. It will be unlocked and opened and you will pass through it. Then it will
swing to and, audibly, be locked behind you.

The locked door that stands between two worlds.

And you who knows them both.

Quite a moment.

NOTES ON CONTRIBUTORS

EUGENE HEIMLER is a psychiatric social worker and as a tutor gives a Human Relations course at London University. His first book *Night of the Mist* (Bodley Head, 1959) relates his experiences in a Nazi concentration camp. This was followed by a second volume *A Link in the Chain* (Bodley Head, 1962) which told the story of his own readjustment to normal, human society.

PAUL IGNOTUS was the editor of a prominent literary monthly in pre-war Hungary. He spent the war years in London working for the B.B.C. After the war he became Press Attaché at the Hungarian Legation in London. In 1949 he went home to Hungary where he was arrested and spent almost seven years in prison. His book, *Political Prisoner* (Routledge and Kegan Paul, 1959) was translated into several European languages. Now he is engaged in writing a biography of Maupassant.

RUSSELL BRADDON first described his experiences in a Japanese prison camp in *The Naked Island* (Werner Laurie, 1952). His latest published work is a biography of his compatriot, Joan Sutherland, the Australian singer (Collins, 1962).

ARTHUR KOESTLER's great work, *The Sleep-walkers* (Hutchinson, 1959) was followed by his impressions of a Far Eastern journey, *The Lotus and the Robot* (Hutchinson, 1960). His new work, *The Act of Creation*, will be published by Hutchinson in 1964. The subtitle of this vast book is : The Art of Discovery and the Discoveries of Art.

KRISHNA NEHRU HUTHEESING is the younger sister of India's Prime Minister. Her autobiography, *With No Regrets* (Oxford University Press, 1944) will be followed by a second instalment of autobiographical writing later this year.

WALTER MUSGRAVE is a pseudonym.

COLIN FRANKLIN is a director of Routledge and Kegan Paul.

JEREMY BRYAN is a pseudonym.